"Dotlich and Cairo have worked with leaders of the world's top corporations as both coaches and teachers. *Action Coaching* summarizes their experiences in a way that makes coaching accessible, practical, and productive."

—Judy Oppenheim, senior vice president, human resources and corporate services, AVID Technology

"This book is a behind-the-scenes look at what two world-class executive coaches actually do with their clients."

—Howard Levine, vice president, business consulting and organization development, Merck & Co., Inc.

"*Action Coaching* shows how the right coach, the right leader, and the right method can lead to improved business results. Coaching is not 'soft': it is one of the most important ways leaders learn to survive and thrive in a world of paradox, speed, and constant change."

—Chris Rice, Global 1000 partner, Arthur Andersen LLP

ACTION
COACHING

ACTION

HOW TO LEVERAGE INDIVIDUAL PERFORMANCE FOR COMPANY SUCCESS

COACHING

DAVID L. DOTLICH   PETER C. CAIRO

JOSSEY-BASS
A Wiley Imprint
www.josseybass.com

Library of Congress Cataloging-in-Publication Data

Dotlich, David Landreth.
    Action coaching : how to leverage individual performance for company success / David L. Dotlich, Peter C. Cairo.
        p.   cm.
    Includes bibliographical references and index.
    ISBN 0-7879-4477-7
    1. Mentoring in business.   I. Cairo, Peter C.   II. Title.
HF5385.D68   1999
658.39124—dc21   99-33631

Printed in the United States of America
FIRST EDITION
HB Printing   10 9 8 7 6 5 4

For Esau Dotlich and Cosma P. Cairo
Our first, and best, coaches

Contents

Preface

In today's organizations, every manager is a coach. Whether you're a top executive or in your first supervisory role, you're being called upon to work with people in ways that no one has prepared you for. As "external" coaches, we are well aware of this fact. We're brought in to coach people the organization has tried and failed to help and people whose development the organization wants to accelerate. Time after time, the people who bring us in say, "We wish we knew how to do what you do."

Although this book won't make you a professional coach, it will help you handle your job's coaching responsibilities in extraordinarily effective ways. We'll share a coaching philosophy and process, as well as some tools that are quite a bit different from the standard coaching approach. We view coaching as a flexible strategy for dealing with a wide range of individual and organizational issues. Creating individual self-awareness is only a beginning, not an end in itself. Whether we're working with a top executive who needs to develop new areas of expertise or a high-potential manager who has a flaw that is decreasing his effectiveness, we frequently move people beyond being self-aware to actually doing things. We coach to facilitate individual development and to link that development to the achievement of organization objectives.

We call our approach Action Coaching. Over the years, we've worked as coaches for a wide variety of organizations, including

Pfizer, Johnson & Johnson, Colgate-Palmolive, Shell Oil, Levi-Strauss, Boeing, BellSouth, The Limited, Daimler-Benz, Merck, Bankers Trust, Nike, AT&T, Arthur Andersen, Sprint, Bank of America, and many other companies. Our Action Coaching experiences with people in these organizations will be referred to throughout the book, but because of the sensitive nature of many of the issues involved, we've usually changed the names of the individuals as well as the organizations.

Whether you're a manager who wants to learn how to coach more effectively, an HR leader who needs a performance-based coaching model, or a top executive who wants to link individual coaching to organizational goals, this book will meet your needs. Using case histories, anecdotes, and a variety of tools and techniques, we'll demonstrate how you can apply the Action Coaching process to your particular situation.

This book has been years in the making. For more than two decades, we each were developing the philosophy and expertise that resulted in our coaching approach. Interestingly, although we developed this philosophy and expertise separately at the beginning, there were remarkable similarities in what we produced. When we began working together about seven years ago, we realized we were kindred coaching spirits. We'd like to briefly share the evolution of our coaching approach with you.

David Speaks

I began my working life as a psychologist and an academic. In 1981, I was a professor at the University of Minnesota when a consulting client, Honeywell, asked me to join the company to help them tackle a number of new areas—quality circles, development of leadership talent, and participative management. Intrigued, I took the position in their organizational development department, assuming that I'd return to academia after a few years.

Under the tutelage of a Honeywell manager, Arnie Kanarick (who is now executive vice president of The Limited), I began making a transition from teaching to learning about the organizational world. In a sense, Arnie was my coach; he gave me feedback, helped me reflect on my experiences, and fostered the performance breakthrough necessary for me to succeed at Honeywell. I became an executive vice president there, and along the way I learned a great deal about how to do with others what Arnie had done with me. I initiated and supervised a number of coaching-related programs at Honeywell, including an innovative project in which we created a corporate award for Honeywell's fifty best coaches.

While working at Honeywell and later at a spun-off computer business, the France-based Groupe Bull, I developed a strong sense of how people should be coached and eventually left the latter company, focusing my efforts on consulting and teaching positions (at the University of Minnesota and University of Michigan Business School). As part of my consulting work for companies such as Shell Oil, Ameritech, and Johnson & Johnson, I implemented the process called Action Learning, which was designed to help people—especially leaders—grow and develop faster and more effectively. In effect, Action Learning created a hybrid world that combined the classroom with real work environments. Learning new skills and concepts in this atmosphere was a training breakthrough for many companies, as documented in *Action Learning* (Jossey-Bass, 1998), a book I coauthored with Jim Noel, another Action Learning proponent.

Although Action Learning usually takes place in teams, individual coaching is often integrated into the process. From these experiences, I developed an approach to coaching that dovetailed with the work Peter had been doing. Together, we created the model that became Action Coaching.

Peter Speaks

As a psychology professor at Columbia University and chairman of their Department of Organizational and Counseling Psychology until 1997, I studied and taught topics such as career decision making and work adjustment. As a result of my research in these areas, I wrote a paper for AT&T in the early 1980s called "Counseling in Business and Industry." This paper generated a great deal of interest at AT&T and resulted in a variety of consulting projects with the company, including working with their psychologists to use assessment center technology to enhance development. Much of my work with AT&T involved coaching executives, though we didn't call it coaching back then.

I was fascinated by the experience and broadened my consulting practice so that I could do more of it. At the same time, however, I knew that I was deficient in knowledge about how organizational systems influence individual performance. I began studying the effect of organizational systems such as leadership practices, strategies, culture, and the like on individuals. Increasingly, I recognized that it was impossible to coach people unless you understood the organization-individual dynamic.

In the early nineties, a colleague of mine at Columbia University, W. Warner Burke, was asked to lead a team that was developing a program for Arthur Andersen to help partners enhance relationships with clients and colleagues. Burke, who is largely credited with creating the field of organizational development, asked me to join the team. It was there that I met David, who was also a member of the team.

In essence, what we ended up doing at Arthur Andersen was coaching partners in ways that required the use of the organization-individual dynamic to which I referred. Working with David, I realized that we shared the same beliefs about how people could be coached effectively—beliefs, I might add, that were at odds with the mainstream coaching methods of the time. David and I formalized our approach, working with companies such as Levi-Strauss, Merck, BellSouth, and Bank of America. We found that our approach, which we termed Action Coaching, was especially effective when people were going through difficult transitions or being asked to develop as leaders.

In 1997 I left Columbia and have been pursuing consulting full time, working with David on many coaching assignments as well as on my own.

Few professional coaches have worked with as many different people in as many different situations as we have. We believe you'll benefit from the diversity and depth of our experience. You'll learn how to deal with a broad spectrum of problems and opportunities. The early chapters will explain our process and how to use it to help individuals and organizations solve problems and capitalize on opportunities. First, however, we need to show you Action Coaching in action.

The initial chapters of this book will give you a detailed description of Action Coaching: what it is, how it works, and how to do it. At this point, however, we simply want you to share our enthusiasm about a coaching concept that will help you help others become more effective managers and leaders.

Acknowledgments

Writing a book requires good coaching from others, and we would like to first acknowledge our many joint clients and colleagues who read the manuscript, provided ideas, or offered themselves up as willing participants for us to hone our skills. At Bank of America, Jim Shanley, Chuck Cooley, Mary Lauria, Corey Seitz, and Steele Alphin are true leaders and learners. Howard Levine at Merck, Marshall Gerber and Jan Johnson at Arthur Andersen, and Deb Himsell at Avon deserve special thanks. Our colleagues at Burke Associates—Bobbie Burke, Janine Waclawski, and Allan Church —have been instrumental in furthering our work.

We are fortunate to be part of a world-class team of coaches and teachers from whom we learn every day: Neil Johnston, Neville Osrin, Debra Noumair, Saletta Boni, Mark Kiefaber, Rod Anderson, Claude Lineberry, Betty Ann Bailey, and Gerry Egan. This book would not have been possible without the energy and commitment of our colleagues at CDR International, who coach us on how we can do it better, faster, and more effectively: Amy Beacom, Kimberly Brinkmeyer, Judy Galloway, Adriel Henderson, Gary Newton, and Nancy Parsons.

Finally, we owe a special debt to our third partner, Stephen Rhinesmith, whose ideas and insights are throughout this book and who manages to set a high standard and make it fun at the same time.

David Speaks

The contributions of many clients, colleagues, and friends can be found throughout this book. First, the leaders with whom it has been my privilege to work: Bob Haas, Pete Jacobi, Gord Shank, John Ermatinger, Donna Goya, and James Capon of Levi-Strauss; and at Sprint, Lynn Badaracco, Len Lauer, Bill Esrey, and Ron LeMay. John Kelly and Grace MacArthur of BPAmoco (ARCO) supported coaching when it wasn't easy to do so. Johnson & Johnson has been a special client for many years and holds a unique place in my heart because it is filled with great leaders and coaches: Bill Weldon, Jeff Nugent, Allen Anderson, Mike Carey, Efram Dlugacz, Peter Tattle, and Roger Fine, among others. Ken Smith of Wafertech and Deborah Barber of Aspect Techology continually challenge my thinking. Other leaders who keep making me a better coach include: at BellSouth, Val Markos and Melanie Cadenhead; at Nike, Danielle Joudene and Kurt Mudd; at Arthur Andersen, Chris Rice and Norbert Becker; and at Tektronix, Jerry Meyer.

Arnie Kanarick, an early and great coach and now executive vice president of The Limited will always be the model for me of how coaching and caring work together. Linda Pierce at Shell Oil has created more than a few defining moments for me. The insights of many executives over the years in the executive programs I have led at the Universities of Michigan, Penn State, and Minnesota have shaped my thinking about what makes coaching successful.

Cedric Crocker of Jossey-Bass is an editor with fairness and fierceness. Some very special colleagues inspire and tolerate me:

Jim Noel, Karen Mailliard, Jerry Meyer, David Walker, Matt Samwick, Judy Oppenheim, Linda Reid, Terry O'Connor, Ed Starincheck, Mike Fruge, Carine Degreve, and Tina Rasmussen. Steve Knecht, Jeremy Raidt, Mary Knecht, and Clare Fitzgerald each give special gifts and have my deep gratitude. And finally, Doug and Carter—for whom any thanks could never be enough.

Peter Speaks

There are many people who have influenced my thinking about coaching and shaped my career. Foremost among them are two former colleagues at Columbia University. Warner Burke helped me understand the importance of organizational context and systems in working with individuals. Roger Myers taught me what I know about the counseling process.

Many clients have afforded me the opportunity to ply my trade. They include Bob Joy of Colgate, Mirian Graddick at AT&T, and Evelyn Rodstein and Wendy Weidenbaum at Bankers Trust.

Finally, special thanks to my wife, Kathy, who makes everything possible, and my children, Danielle, Justin, and Megan, who give my life purpose.

June 1999   David L. Dotlich
                                                 Portland, Oregon

                                                 Peter C. Cairo
                                                 Bearsville, New York

The Authors

David L. Dotlich has been involved with planned organizational change in academics, business, government, and consulting for twenty years. He is a consultant in organizational change, executive coaching, and senior leadership learning issues to the top management of Johnson & Johnson, Levi-Strauss, Bank of America, BellSouth, Sprint, Nike, The Limited, Merck, Arthur Andersen, ARCO, and other companies. He is a certified psychologist in the areas of career development, life planning, and numerous psychological inventories. He is coauthor, with Jim Noel, of *Action Learning: How the World's Best Companies Are Re-Creating Their Leadership and Themselves* (Jossey-Bass, 1998).

From 1986 until 1992, Dotlich was an executive vice president of Groupe Bull, a $7 billion computer manufacturing business headquartered in Paris, with forty-five thousand employees worldwide. He was responsible for all internal and external communication, including the award-winning advertising campaign KNOW BULL, and for human resource and quality improvement activities throughout the world. The emphasis was on leadership training, compensation, and recruitment programs needed to reduce cycle time, control costs, and shift a large hardware manufacturer quickly into new businesses such as services, software, and consulting.

Until 1986, Dotlich was vice president of human resources for Honeywell. Responsible for worldwide training, selection, affirmative action, and research, he spearheaded the formation of

Honeywell's management development strategy and their Corporate Conference and Training Center. He also helped lead such corporatewide projects as One Honeywell; the concept was to present a unified product offering to customers from various divisions. He also conducted the Honeywell Job and Relationship Study, which surveyed 5,700 managers worldwide and identified how effective leaders develop and create winning environments for people.

Before joining Honeywell, Dotlich was on the faculty of the University of Minnesota, teaching in the Business School and the Department of Communication. His teaching and research focused on the impact of organizational culture in producing effective leaders, with special emphasis on women and minorities. His consulting company designed change programs for clients such as IBM, the Federal Reserve Bank, 3M, and the Farm Credit System.

Dotlich's interest in people development began with a first position as a social worker in the Cincinnati inner city. While completing a master's degree in race relations at the University of Witwatersrand in Johannesburg, South Africa, he conducted survey research on racial attitudes in the African townships. After returning to the United States, he joined the U.S. Department of Commerce as a training director and was assigned to Minneapolis. While there, he completed an additional master's degree at the University of Minnesota, where he also received his doctorate.

Dotlich has taught regularly in the executive development programs at the University of Michigan and the University of Minnesota. At Minnesota he designed the highly successful "Leading Human Resources in the 90s" executive program. At Michigan, he developed the Change Leadership Consortium, which brings together line managers from six Fortune 500 companies to develop as change agents in their respective organizations. He is on the ASTD National Issues Committee, the board of directors of Schmidt Industries, and Ash Creek Venture Fund.

Peter C. Cairo, former chair of Columbia University's Department of Organizational and Counseling Psychology, is a consultant who specializes in the areas of leadership development, executive coaching, and organization effectiveness. He is an adjunct professor of psychology at Columbia University, where he recently completed a twenty-year career as a full-time member of the faculty.

At Columbia, Cairo's responsibilities involved oversight of the graduate training programs in the department. He taught courses in career development, assessment, group dynamics, and counseling techniques. He pioneered a course in organizational psychology that involved the application of methods for assessing and facilitating career and professional development in business settings. He also served on the editorial board of the *Journal of Vocational Behavior*.

Cairo's own research focused on career development and work adjustment. He has published numerous articles, book chapters, and reports on topics such as counseling in business and industry, career adjustment in the workplace, assessing adult career development, and using assessment center methodology to promote the development of high-potential managers. His current research interests include the effects of managerial self-awareness on performance, the use of assessment techniques for enhancing leadership development, and the application of traditional models of organizational change to professional services firms.

Among Cairo's recent clients is AT&T, where he served as primary consultant to executives and leadership teams on organization changes associated with mergers, acquisitions, and restructuring. He is a consultant and coach for partners at Arthur Andersen; a member of the faculty of the Executive Leadership Program at Merck, where he also provides coaching for executives; and a coach and consultant for executives at Colgate-Palmolive, Bankers Trust, and the law firm of Fried, Frank, Harris, Shriver and Jacobson.

Cairo is a member of the American Psychological Association, the American Psychological Society, and the American Society for Training and Development. He is a licensed psychologist in the state of New York.

Both authors, along with Stephen Rhinesmith, are partners in CDR International, a global consulting firm that helps companies implement strategy through executive learning and coaching. CDR International's partners and principals are involved in in-house senior executive programs worldwide for companies such as Bank of America, Levi-Strauss, Merck, BellSouth, Sprint, Citigroup, and Arthur Andersen. Both Dotlich and Cairo can be reached at www.cdr-intl.com.

ACTION
COACHING

Introduction

There's a reason why *action* modifies *coaching* in our title. Action takes place when we coach people. Specifically, people move from self-awareness to improved performance, and individual performance objectives are aligned with organizational goals.

Let's start with the second point. Other coaching methods may result in performance improvement. People may be coached in developing better communication skills, and as a result they're able to give their people clearer direction that helps them work faster and better. But what if improved communication skills is way down on an organization's list of priorities for this individual? What if management feels that a quantum leap in performance would take place if this person became more astute about organizational politics? Or what if this individual's inability to develop is hampered more by the corporate culture than by internal issues?

Unlike other coaching methods, the purpose of Action Coaching goes far beyond providing a personal growth opportunity. Although that may be part of it, broader company needs are always considered. Coaching, to be effective for both the individual and the organization, has to manage a delicate balancing act between the two. Sometimes, individuals see their job and career growth in ways that clash with the ways the organization needs them to develop. As coaches, we try to help our clients reconcile this conflict.

We might help them see or do things differently so that what once was a conflict now becomes a manageable paradox.

This leads us to a simple definition of our process: *Action Coaching is a process that fosters self-awareness and leads to the motivation to change, as well as the guidance needed if change is to take place in ways that meet individual and organizational performance needs.*

Moving from self-awareness to improved performance is a critical feature of Action Coaching. How many times have you heard someone complain (or complained yourself) that "coaching might help someone become a better person but not a better performer." People who are coached might gain personal career insights but often fail to improve performance.

Action Coaching has four clearly focused change goals:

Self-awareness. A client gains a better understanding of his attitudes and behaviors, strengths and weaknesses.

Performance improvement. A client improves his performance in a way that contributes to his effectiveness in growing a business, for example, by improving profitability, increasing revenues, expanding market share, increasing employee productivity, or exceeding customer expectations.

Performance breakthrough. A client raises his personal or job performance to an entirely new level, one that constitutes a significant change in his own and others' perceptions of his capabilities and potential.

Transformation. A client makes a fundamental change in behavior, attitude, values, and basic emotional intelligence that opens up new possibilities for him and his organization in the future (see Exhibit I.1).

In the planning stages of the coaching process, we work with people to define what they want and need to achieve. For some people, performance improvement is fine. For others, nothing less

Exhibit I.1. The Four Levels of Coaching Goals.

than transformation will do. These goals are determined not only by the coach and her client but in conjunction with the organization (with input from a boss, HR people, top management, and so on). This ensures that the action that takes place—the change in an individual's attitude and behaviors or the development of specific skills—is linked to business strategies and imperatives.

Now let's look at an example of someone who was coached with transformation as his change goal.

Transformation from Plant Manager to President

Charles, the recently promoted president of a large electronics subsidiary, hired us to coach him with modest goals in mind. There was no big crisis that prompted his call for coaching. Charles had been a plant manager for many years, and he was questioning his abilities; his most immediate concern was improving his relationship with his boss. As a result of our coaching, he discovered that his desire to please his boss was interfering with his ability to stake out his own identity as a leader and challenge decisions that he thought were misguided. Although this insight helped him become more independent and strengthened his decision-making ability, Charles simply became more self-aware.

The next time he brought us in, he had a more ambitious goal in mind. He was concerned about both his own performance as the president of the company and his ability to work with and raise the performance level of his executive team. The competition in his industry was intensifying and he was justifiably worried. Charles understood that there was still a lot of plant manager left in him—that he lacked the vision, the image, and the effectiveness of a true president.

From the start, we set envelope-pushing goals for both Charles and his team—goals that required significant behavioral changes. These goals revolved around the way in which Charles managed his team: he tolerated excuses, complaining, and back-biting conflicts. Charles saw himself as a participatory leader, but in fact he was often a weak-willed leader. His major goal was to transform himself from a leader in name to a leader in deed. We reasoned that if he could craft a strong vision for the company and inspire and motivate his people more effectively, the organization would be able to hold off or even gain on the competition. By providing Charles with honest feedback from a variety of sources—we sat in on team meetings and gave him our impressions of what we had observed—we "shocked" him into taking action. By benchmarking other leaders and leading companies and showing Charles how they had transformed themselves, we gave him models to adapt to his own situation. We also encouraged Charles to rehearse his new role with us, and we pointed out how his new attitude and actions might produce desired business gains.

In the year we worked with Charles, he became a very different sort of leader. The pleasant but unconfident pleaser we had met with initially vanished. In his place was a decisive, charismatic visionary. Charles had not only reorganized the business, entered new markets, and reprioritized resources in a strategic manner but he had gained the respect and dedication of his management team.

Would Charles have grown into his role without our coaching? Perhaps. But at the very least, Action Coaching accelerated the process. Charles had been willing and motivated to change from the very beginning, but he was unwilling to take the risk without a plan and a certainty that his personal changes would positively affect the company. As we helped him reframe his beliefs, challenged his assumptions, rehearsed his behaviors, and listened to his fears, we made sure that Charles never lost sight of the overarching business strategy and objectives. This kept Charles focused, moving forward, and willing to take risks. The payoff was transformation, both for himself and his organization.

Parable of the Ugly Tie

Like Charles, many of our clients are highly ambitious in their goals. Although some may begin with simple self-awareness objectives, once they see the power of the process they are eager for more. In our fast-changing global marketplace, self-awareness or even performance improvement isn't always enough to meet performance goals or achieve desired business results. Breakthroughs and transformations are essential.

Let us tell you a parable that illustrates this point. You see a friend and muster the courage to tell him that his tie is ugly. As a result, he changes ties and looks better for it. He thanks you for your feedback and vows never to wear ugly ties again. And the next time you see him, he is wearing a very attractive tie. But his shirt is a pink polyester nightmare. Once again you give him feedback and he thanks you and changes his shirt, but the next time you see him you realize he's wearing two-toned, imitation leather shoes. No matter how aware he becomes of one ugly aspect of his wardrobe, there's always some other aspect that both you and he have neglected to address.

Now let's put this story in terms of our four Action Coaching goals:

Self-awareness. He realizes he wears ugly ties.

Performance improvement. He changes ties to something nicer.

Performance breakthrough. He changes his entire wardrobe.

Transformation. He tailors his wardrobe to reflect who he wants to be and the impact he wants to have on others.

If all you do is tell someone that a particular article of clothing is ugly, you'll never get beyond performance improvement. Sometimes this is enough, but often coaching goes deeper and connects with issues beyond who people are as individuals to how they affect larger business issues and concerns.

Types of Action Coaches

Who needs to learn how to coach in the manner we're describing? The facetious answer—all managers—is probably closer to the truth than most people think. We're finding that organizations are increasingly reluctant to ship their managers to external or even internal universities for "improvement" or to conduct massive executive education programs. In companies throughout the world, there's a growing recognition that programs need to be targeted at the individual—that people aren't going to change negative behaviors or develop new skills unless they receive feedback, reflect on what they hear, have someone to talk to about their issues, and help them construct a plan to deal with them. In other words, they need to be coached.

As a result, companies are starting to recognize that coaching is a core competency for managers and that managers can be far more effective if they can coach their people from a framework of individual performance and organizational goals. A coach is no longer synonymous with a tweedy-looking psychologist who is brought into a company to deal with a troubled employee. Think about which of the following Action Coaching roles fits what you do and who you are:

- *Manager coaches.* The old notion of a manager was a no-nonsense boss who didn't deal with the soft issues. Not so many years ago, managers wouldn't touch issues such as individual purpose and values versus results. Today such issues are crucial. For one thing, the role of the manager has expanded as the number of managers per company has shrunk. For another, self-reliant workforces require individual managers to do more of their own problem solving. Coaching allows managers to do more with less. In addition, managers can no longer motivate without getting into both the head and hearts of their people. Coaching helps managers do exactly that.

- *Executive coaches.* Many executives are using coaching to train and mentor future leaders; they're also employing it as a way to develop key competencies in their direct reports. At the same time, they're determining when coaching is appropriate, deciding who should be a coach (external or internal), and setting coaching goals for individuals that link to desired business results. For example, at Sprint a new leadership model for executives cites coaching and developing people as a key criteria for success in that company.

- *Peer coaches.* As organizations flatten and the lines between functions and titles blur — and as individuals are increasingly working together in self-directed teams — the need for peers to coach each other has intensified. It's not always possible to go to a boss for help; co-workers are much more likely to have the time and inclination to assist a fellow worker who is having problems or wants to develop in new ways. All they need are accessible coaching skills.

- *Specially trained internal coaches.* These people often reside in the HR group, and their mission is to coach whoever needs assistance. Like school counselors, they exist because organizations recognize that the high-pressure, competitive environment and confusing issues will produce people with problems and unmet goals. Permanent coaches such as these are terrific generalists, able to handle a wide range of coaching issues. Today, in companies such as Johnson & Johnson, Levi-Strauss, and Bank of America, a principal role for their human resource professionals is performance improvement coach.

• *External coaches.* These still exist, though they tend to be more specialized than in the past. Organizations usually hire such coaches for specific purposes: to develop high-potentials, to handle politically charged situations (where an internal coach wouldn't have the objectivity or platform to do a good job), to work on leadership development issues such as accelerating the business skills of individuals or groups, or to deal with complicated or delicate problems (a highly talented but out-of-control executive). In other words, external coaches have the specialized expertise that other people might not have.

Incidentally, you will notice that we nearly always use the word *client* when referring to the person being coached. We recognize that this term doesn't always fit; for example, managers do not refer to their direct reports as clients. Our problem was that no other word we could think of made sense in all the coaching relationships we described. (No one we know uses the term *coachee!*) So we settled on *client* and hope the reader understands that we mean this in the broadest sense. (See Exhibit I.2.)

Action Coaching Attributes

The requirement for coaching expertise varies, depending on your role in the organization. This book will provide what you need to know to develop coaching competency from basic to expert levels. Still, you may have doubts. How do you know whether you have what it takes to coach effectively?

Exhibit I.2. Types of Coaches.

Type of Coach	Coaching Task
Manager-coaches	Motivate their employees' heads *and* hearts, encouraging them to do more with less
Executive coaches	Use coaching to mentor future leaders; set leaders' coaching goals that link to business results
Peer coaches	Coach others (peers); used in flatter organizations that use self-directed teams
Specially trained internal coaches	Company employees, often in HR, who coach leaders and employees on a variety of issues
External coaches	Usually hired for specific purposes (for example, high-potentials, politically charged situations, executives), bring in specialized expertise or objectivity

We've found that coaching is a highly learnable skill, especially for people who possess certain traits. Before turning to the next chapter, we'd like you to review the following list of what we refer to as Action Coaching Attributes (ACAs) (see Exhibit I.3). Although some of these attributes are useful for any type of coaching, a number are specific to Action Coaching. Effective Action Coaches require the right personal and behavioral qualities, a perspective on the organization as well as the individual, and a strong results orientation. Place a plus mark next to the attributes you think you have and a minus next to the ones you lack.

How many plus marks did you make? Here's what the marks mean:

0–4 = Lots of work to do; but remember that Action Coaching is teachable.

Exhibit I.3. Action Coaching Attributes Checklist.

Personal Qualities	Yes	No
I am empathetic and have the ability to put myself in someone else's shoes.	❏	❏
I am flexible and willing to adapt my approach to individual situations rather than getting locked into one way of doing things.	❏	❏
I am willing to listen deeply and hear the other person's underlying concerns, fears, aspirations, and ambitions.	❏	❏
Behavior Qualities		
I am able to provide feedback clearly and without judgment.	❏	❏
I have the ability to motivate others, that is, to identify the particular need or dream that drives an individual and tap into it as a source of motivation.	❏	❏
I am effective at setting "stretch" goals for people — goals that are challenging but achievable.	❏	❏
Organization Perspective		
I can balance the needs of an individual with organizational requirements.	❏	❏
I am a big-picture thinker who can put situations in a larger context so people don't get bogged down by details.	❏	❏
I am good at integrating different ideas, techniques, and people to solve problems.	❏	❏
Results Orientation		
I hold people accountable for results and require that they move past understanding to accomplishment.	❏	❏
I am good at developing plans that achieve objectives and produce results.	❏	❏
I can pinpoint the behavior and attitudinal changes that are necessary to achieve specific business results.	❏	❏

5–8 = You're off to a good start but still have a way to go.

9–12 = You have a strong foundation on which to continue building your skills.

Now look at where your plus marks cluster. Where are your gaps? Do you need to focus more on personal qualities or the behaviors necessary to be an effective Action Coach? How effective are you at putting people's needs in the context of your organization? Do you focus enough on results?

This book will help you focus on areas that are most important for you to develop. Action Coaching ultimately requires all of what we've discussed already, plus other tools, techniques, and approaches that we'll discuss later on. We begin by describing what we mean by Action Coaching and why it should matter to you.

Part I

Getting Started as an Action Coach

1

Action Coaching: A Brief Introduction

Each day you face the challenge of helping people adapt to ambitious new workplace requirements. Perhaps you're a manager attempting to encourage a direct report to become more openminded and innovative. Or you might be a top executive struggling to convince a high-potential person to take more risks. No matter what your position or assignment might be, you're being asked to motivate people to change dramatically and to change fast.

But the challenge doesn't end there. You must lead individuals along organization-sanctioned paths; they have to develop competencies that the organization deems crucial or cease behaviors that were once accepted in the culture and now are counterproductive. If that isn't enough of a challenge, you're faced with people who may be aware that they should change but don't have the foggiest notion of how they can do so within a particular job or working for a particular person. Equally problematic, many of the men and women you're dealing with are confused by issues that go beyond job issues. They're searching for meaningful work and questioning whether their job (or any job in their field) can give it to them.

If you're like many of the people we've worked with, you've tried to deal with these complex issues in all sorts of ways. You've used internal training courses, outside executive development programs, and many other methods. You may even have brought in coaches to assist you. The odds are that you were dissatisfied with the results of all these approaches; none are flexible; none have either an action component or the ability to link individual and organizational goals.

Action Coaching is uniquely geared to the developmental challenges that managers, human resources professionals, and leaders face today. Whether you want to coach your peers, direct reports, or high-potentials, you can benefit from the process presented here. It's a process that you can master and use, not only to help your people meet ambitious and complex professional development goals but to help your organization achieve key business objectives.

That's promising a lot, and we'll back up that promise with some examples, definitions, and comparisons to other coaching methods a bit later in the chapter. But first, we'd like you to evaluate your own coaching needs. To get a sense of whether Action Coaching might help you and your company, answer the questions in Exhibit 1.1.

Exhibit 1.1. Are You Coaching-Challenged?

	Yes	No
1. Do you feel frustrated when you attempt to help others improve their performance? Do they seem to ignore any advice or ideas you offer and resent any sanctions you threaten them with or impose?	❏	❏
2. Does it seem that you can reach people intellectually and explain what they're doing wrong but you can't reach them at a deeper level where behavioral changes occur?	❏	❏
3. Do you have a number of people who work for or with you who for one reason or another are performing significantly below their potential? Have you failed to help them fulfill that potential using incentives and other motivational tools?	❏	❏
4. Do you find that some of your subordinates or team members have been very successful for years with	❏	❏

	Yes	No

a certain work style and refuse to change that style
even though it's no longer as successful as it once was?

5. Does it drive you crazy trying to get people to
recognize that the rules of the game have changed? Do
they resist new policies, procedures, and cultural shifts?

6. Are there people in your group who say one thing
but do another—who verbally assure you and others
that they value diversity, global thinking, and
teamwork and yet consistently contradict what they
say with their actions?

7. Do you manage or work with people who could use
a figurative kick in the head—who are skilled but
stubborn, clinging to beliefs and practices no matter
what you or anyone else say or do?

8. Does it seem impossible to get certain people to see
the big picture or at least view a situation from a fresh
perspective? Does it seem that if you could get them to
see things differently, they might begin to act differently?

9. Do people you work with or for you seem to view
ambiguity, uncertainty, and paradox like they're a
plague? Do they have trouble making decisions when
the answers aren't crystal clear?

10. Does your group or team struggle mightily with any
type of transition? Do they have one foot in the old
paradigm and the other foot in the new paradigm?

11. Do you ever wish you could accelerate the process
by which people change? Does it seem that it'll take
forever for them to acquire new skills, attitudes,
behaviors (and that you don't have forever)?

12. Are coworkers, direct reports, and others willing to
try new approaches and open to new ideas but, in doing
so, go off in a million unproductive directions? Do they
make changes in the way they work but not the changes
you or management want?

The more yes answers you have, the more likely it is that this unique approach to coaching will be helpful to you.

Action Coaching Defined

Our definition of Action Coaching is simple: *Action Coaching is a process that fosters self-awareness and that results in the motivation to change, as well as the guidance needed if change is to take place in ways that meet organizational needs.*

This definition raises the how questions: How do you motivate someone to move beyond self-awareness and do something about it? How do you make sure that someone changes in ways that have a positive impact on business results rather than in ways that only foster individual career goals? Let's answer these questions by describing the four essential elements of Action Coaching and how they foster personal development in organizational directions.

First, *self-awareness is linked with business results*. During the first or second meeting between coach and client, goals are set that join how an individual perceives the need to change with the organization's perception of the need to change. These two perceptions must be discussed and reconciled. The client may think his only task is to stop being such a harsh critic of his direct reports, whereas the management mandate may be broader, suggesting that he must develop a wider range of people management skills. Because individual and organizational perceptions often clash, they need to be aired from the start and goals set that take both into consideration.

Second, *an action plan is put in place*. Action Coaching plans are clear and substantial; they ask people to accomplish specific workplace tasks or set milestones to determine whether they are making progress. Action Coaching requires clients to document and report progress in trying new behaviors and learning new skills. Coaches' recommendations can affect a client's future with the company, both positively and negatively. The coach makes this clear, and a client understands that she will be held accountable for taking certain agreed-upon actions.

Third, *the level of achievement is set based on organizational need.* Sometimes a person needs to be coached simply to help her be aware of a tendency to lose her temper with inexperienced employees. The organizational goal of decreasing turnover among this group can be achieved if the manager learns to be a bit more tolerant. Other times, nothing less than a complete transformation of attitudes and behaviors will suffice. For this reason, we set one of four goals for clients: *self-awareness, performance improvement, performance breakthrough,* or *transformation.* If a manager is to help her group achieve objectives that demand a performance breakthrough, she must work on developing in ways that go beyond incremental improvements.

Fourth, *the process is structured and provides proven tools.* Coaching has been rightly criticized for being a seat-of-the-pants methodology; it often lacks a formal strategy, tactics, or goals. Action Coaching unfolds in a logical, orderly manner. Not only is there a beginning, middle, and end to the process but a wide variety of tools and techniques are available to facilitate the process. This well-organized, highly resourced approach avoids the uncertainties and vague outcomes that plague other coaching approaches. It sets a path for both coach and client to keep moving toward the goal rather than becoming stuck and frustrated or going off in the wrong direction. (See Exhibit 1.2.)

Action Coaching Differentiated

Traditional coaching is typically derived from the model of a therapist-patient relationship. Although the style of traditional coaches may vary somewhat, the goal is usually self-awareness. The assumption is that because the individual is in business, he or she must be highly motivated. Traditional coaching is usually conducted through relatively unstructured interactions; it also lacks an action or organizational linkage component. This is not to say that traditional coaching is all bad. In fact, the goal of raising self-awareness is important in Action Coaching, and there are similarities to

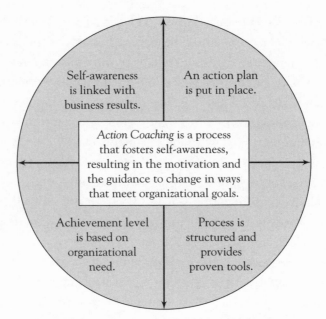

Self-awareness
is linked with
business results.

An action plan
is put in place.

Action Coaching is a process
that fosters self-awareness,
resulting in the motivation and
the guidance to change in ways
that meet organizational goals.

Achievement level
is based on
organizational
need.

Process is
structured and
provides
proven tools.

Exhibit 1.2. Action Coaching Defined.

traditional coaching in the way we go about doing that. If you can't help someone become aware of a behavior or attitude he needs to change or an area in which he needs to develop strength, you won't be able to motivate him to take any kind of meaningful action. That said, let's look at the differences as they are illustrated in Exhibit 1.3.

These differences emerged over time, and a brief history of how they emerged will help you understand their significance. In the last decade coaching has become if not ubiquitous then certainly commonplace. Organizations routinely bring in coaches — usually a hybrid of therapist and business consultant — to work with problematic executives. Typically, coaches help their clients become aware of negative behaviors and attitudes that affect their performance, sometimes linking these behaviors and attitudes to personal issues from their past. The theory is that this self-awareness begets changes in behaviors and attitudes, thereby eliminating the obstacle that is hurting their performance.

Exhibit 1.3. From Traditional Coaching to Action Coaching.

From Traditional Coaching	⇨	To Action Coaching
• Therapist-patient relationship	⇨	• Business relationship
• One-size-fits-all approach to development	⇨	• Individualized approach, tailored to the person's needs
• Self-awareness as an end	⇨	• Uses self-awareness as a means to change behavior
• Focused primarily on personal insights, not action	⇨	• Focused on translating insights into action toward organizational results
• Unstructured approach and interactions	⇨	• Specific strategy and action planning leads to performance breakthroughs
• Focus on individual only; little link to organizational realities and obstacles in changing behavior	⇨	• Links individual and organizational issues; sets coaching in context of environmental goals and obstacles to change

This type of coaching intervention is a relatively new phenomenon—part of a larger trend of "individualization." Individualized education is rapidly making its way into training and executive education. Intranets, computer simulations, and other electronic tools are facilitating customized learning for specific skill and developmental requirements. Training and development courses are becoming increasingly geared to smaller groups of people with specialized needs.

Coaching has gained favor as an extension of this trend. Rather than assuming that the development of managers and leaders occurs naturally, organizations are bringing in coaches to protect their investment. More than ever before, human assets are of critical importance to companies. As the playing field levels in areas such as technology and information, the competitive edge goes to the company with the highest-performing people.

Traditional coaching, however, is of limited effectiveness in this regard. Although it often does a great job of making people aware of their flaws and the issues holding them back, it doesn't help them take action. The issues are too complex today for a coaching intervention to do much more than help people learn more about themselves. This is a worthy goal in and of itself, but it doesn't give people a mechanism for dealing with the real-world ambiguities and paradoxes in their business environment, nor does it give them a strategy for putting their new self-knowledge to work to achieve individual performance and organizational goals.

To give you a sense of how Action Coaching operates differently, let's look at a common problem that mandates coaching. Assume that you have a direct report who tends to overreact under pressure, and this makes it difficult for people to work with him when deadlines or major projects are involved. You and your boss aren't as concerned with this individual's overreaction as with his inability to grow and nurture his people; this is what the company feels is a crucial competency for its future.

Certainly you would help this executive understand the roots of his overreacting behaviors, as any coach would. But you would also put this problem in a broader context, soliciting feedback from numerous sources so that you'd uncover the direction in which he really needs to develop (your assumptions about this direction may not be correct or may need some refining). You would then create a plan for this executive that would require a performance breakthrough; the improvement that seemed necessary at first glance would be insufficient. You would also look at organizational issues that might hamper the executive's efforts to achieve this breakthrough (such as a culture that doesn't support nurturing behaviors) and develop strategies for overcoming these obstacles.

The business and organizational context is critical in Action Coaching. We're sure you've seen managers emerge from coaching and attempt to work hard on their motivational skills, their relationships with bosses and subordinates, and their communication capabilities. But as dedicated as they may be to self-improvement, they're thwarted by factors outside of who they are: the lack of agreement on a business direction within their team, skill gaps among the people implementing programs for them, faulty systems that prevent people from obtaining needed knowledge or rewarding them for changes made, and a million other things. The Action Coaching process links who people are (their skills, their flaws, their tendencies) with their environmental realities and their organization's strategies and goals.

Coaching in Context: An Example

We'd like to give you a sense of the type of people we coach and the context in which we coach them. Their behavioral problems and development issues are complex, to say the least. Coaching, to be effective, needs to deal with the complexities—with the psychological factors, the organizational roadblocks, the personal career goals, and the overriding group (team, department, organization) objectives.

Typically, your impetus to coach someone comes from one of three sources: (1) you want to develop a high-potential person, (2) you want to help someone adapt to a new or changing environment, or (3) you want to raise an individual's performance level to meet expectations. (See Exhibit 1.4.)

The issues you'll grapple with vary, depending on the catalyst for your coaching. If you're trying to develop a high-potential, you may be coaching someone who is performing well and has no behavioral problems; you're searching for a way to help him see the big picture or to change his attitude about his job. If you're helping someone adapt to a new environment, you may be coaching your client to think globally or to stop behaving in a way that is inappropriate to a new culture. Raising performance levels can involve

Exhibit 1.4. Contexts for Coaching.

Develop High-Potentials	Adapt to New Environmental Realities	Raise Performance
Helping the person	Helping the person	Helping the person
• Maximize his or her potential	• Adapt to changing external demands	• Raise his or her performance to meet expectations
• Succeed in a developmental assignment	• Adapt to changing business trends	• Address a performance problem
• Adjust to a new position	• Transition to requirements of the organizational culture	• Address a problematic situation

anything from dealing with psychological obstacles to evaluating relationships with bosses, direct reports, and customers.

All this makes coaching a complex business. To give you a sense of how Action Coaching handles the complexities, we'd like to tell you about a dynamic executive who was having trouble meeting her boss's expectations.

Case Example: Vivian

Vivian was a senior executive for a fashionable clothing store chain. Overweight, middle-aged, and highly demanding, she was the head of merchandising and buying. Although Vivian demanded perfection from her mostly GenX buyers, she demanded it with flair. She insisted that reports be stapled in a certain way and that meetings start at a ridiculously early hour. That was a bit off-putting, but she had earned the respect of her buyers and her boss.

For eight years Vivian had worked for the same woman, and their relationship was strong and synergistic. Then Vivian's boss left, and a young, male hot-shot was recruited from another company to take her place. He acted as if Vivian had just immigrated from another planet. He asked, "Why can't she be more flexible? Why is she so stuck in her approach that during brainstorming sessions I know exactly what she's going to say? Given that we're a highly fashion-conscious company, how can she present herself so poorly? Why can't she get some new clothes, lose some weight, and be more outgoing at fashion events?"

This was a combustible mix of questions. Not only was there man-woman tension but there were generational tensions, too. On top of that, the major clash in leadership styles, the entrenched loyalty of Vivian's subordinates, and the strong political support from different camps that Vivian had cultivated and that her new boss enjoyed resulted in, overnight, Vivian's change from high-performer to low-performer in serious trouble. Defusing the tension required an expert in emotional explosives.

Vivian was struggling to adapt to a new boss's expectations. When her organization called us in, they didn't want us to encourage Vivian to cave in and do what her new boss required. The last thing they wanted was for Vivian to feel like they were holding a gun to her head or that she had to become someone she was not.

It was clear that the goal was for Vivian to improve her relationship with her new boss. The organization had ambitious strategies that they were counting on Vivian and her boss to help execute. To do so, they needed to enjoy the same synergistic relationship as the one between Vivian and her former boss.

Part of our coaching work was designed to let Vivian explore why she was having so much trouble with her new boss's requirements. It turned out that she was at a life stage where she had begun questioning her career commitment. She wanted to do so many other things—write, paint, have children—that she was feeling trapped. It wasn't simply that her old boss was gone. Her performance might have deteriorated no matter who was in charge.

At the same time, her new boss was exacerbating her problems. Vivian still liked many things about her job and the company, and she had amazing talent. We opened the lines of communication between Vivian and her boss. We facilitated dialogues between them that moved the personal invective off to the side and focused on the real business issues. Gradually, Vivian began to understand that her midlife crisis was responsible for some of her negative behaviors and that her boss was right to call her on them. Her boss also began to understand that Vivian commanded unusual loyalty and respect among her peers and coworkers and possessed skills that were invaluable to the organization and that he himself lacked.

None of this would have been effective, however, without Vivian grasping what was at stake from a business perspective. Much of our coaching revolved around giving Vivian feedback about how people were depending on her—how the organization and her own group had a lot riding on her ability to work productively with her new boss. Vivian was motivated to improve her performance because she recognized the overarching organizational need for improvement and also because we had constructed a plan that would allow her to deal with her personal issues as well as meet performance goals. Taking the whole person into consideration—all the career and personal "stuff" combined with the business requirements—is what Action Coaching is all about.

Why Action Coaching Is Effective

To a certain extent, we said why Action Coaching is effective when we defined and differentiated our coaching approach. The process of linking individual self-awareness and organizational issues, the formal structure of the process, the focus on one of four goal achievement levels, and the development of an action plan—all enhance the efficacy of coaching.

But let's bring the discussion down to the trenches. Coaching people can often be like pulling teeth with a slippery pair of pliers—but not always. When you're working with someone and suddenly they "get it" and actually change before your eyes—and change in ways that benefit both the individual and the organization—you see how effective Action Coaching is. Let's look at four crucial elements that are built into the process.

Eye-Opening Perception

Believing is seeing is an Action Coaching maxim. An individual believes something is true about himself or his workplace and then selectively perceives evidence to support this viewpoint. Action Coaching jars perceptions by confronting individuals about their beliefs, using multirater (360-degree) feedback, benchmarking, shadowing (the coach observes the client in work situations and confronts him about his behaviors), and many other techniques. Other forms of coaching may involve some confrontation and personal revelations, but Action Coaching goes further and opens people's eyes to the world around them. Epiphanies take many forms, and the cumulative effect is what pushes people to change and grow. To give you a sense of what we mean, we've created a list of different experiences our clients have had and that resulted in eye-opening perception:

Hearing not only your boss but your direct reports and customers tell you that what you believe to be your tolerant attitude is actually passive-aggressive behavior

Testing a new behavior in a work situation as part of an experiment and sharing your feelings about how others reacted to you with your coach

Visiting another company and talking to someone who had to deal with the same difficult workplace changes that you're now going through

Being confronted by your coach and told that the situation has reached the point where if you don't learn to develop in

a certain way, you will no longer be on track for a leadership
position

Receiving information from your coach about the CEO's vision
for the company, revealing why certain policy changes have
been made and the need for you to make dramatic changes in
the way you manage

Emphasis on Doing

As much as people may learn about seeing things differently, they
also need to act on that perception. People are not allowed to go
through the process and merely articulate how they've changed;
they need to show they've changed. Action Coaching relationships always involve a contract for behavioral change between
the coach and the person being coached. Sometimes the action
is relatively simple, and Action Coaching focuses on rehearsing
that action: making a call to a difficult customer, practicing confronting a problematic employee, or establishing a new, more productive relationship with a peer. Even after the formal Action
Coaching program is finished, follow-up steps are still in place to
ensure accountability.

For harried and time-challenged managers today, this behavioral accountability makes all the difference in the world. We've all
seen people go through outstanding executive education programs,
resolve to make changes in keeping with what they've been taught,
but fail to do so because the real world intervenes. Although they
have the best of intentions, their resolve melts in the face of too
many things to do and not enough time; they slip back into comfortable old behaviors without thinking. Action Coaching usually
stops this from happening and calls people on it if it does.

Recognition of Complexity in the Business World

The new business world is painted in shades of gray rather than the
traditional black and white.

Professor Ron Heifetz of Harvard University has identified the difference between *adaptive* and *technical* leadership, and Action Coaching is designed to deal with the former.[1] Technical challenges have clear answers. For example, a technical problem might be solved by spending more money, or a new customer service requirement might be addressed by adding personnel. Certain technical requirements are important to every business, and they demand leaders who can come up with clear, direct responses.

Adaptive challenges are messier. Clear answers are elusive, and people may have done nothing in their careers to prepare them to deal with the challenges. People in leadership positions, for instance, are used to dealing with technical issues from position power. Now they are being asked to handle adaptive matters and to do so through influence rather than position. Examples of adaptive issues include moving innovation around various global organizational offices, helping people redefine the customer service chain so they can do things differently, changing a company's culture, and helping people face and accept the reality of technology and its impact on their role.

To work with these issues effectively, people may need to do all sorts of unfamiliar things. Instead of making decisions themselves, they must involve others — toss them the ball and wait patiently for them to toss it back. They must move forward without a set-in-stone plan, managing as they go. They also must learn to work with people's frustration when there are no easy answers and subordinates feel like they're drowning in ambiguity and paradox.

Action Coaching functions as a form of support when individuals are struggling with adaptive issues. As part of the process, these people express how difficult it is working outside their comfort zone; they talk about their uncertainties and doubts about their own capabilities. Action Coaching helps them become more

[1] Heifetz, R. A., *Leadership Without Easy Answers* (Cambridge, Mass.: Belknap Press, 1994).

comfortable with new ways of leading and working; it provides the feedback, information, reflection, and experiences that give people the chance to explore how they lead, manage, and work and whether their style fits the new realities of their environment.

Tailor-Made for Transitions

Even though people face all sorts of transitions, one of the most troubling is job change among senior-level managers. People have always made this type of transition, but they have never faced the pressure to make it as quickly as they do today. Also, people are making bigger jumps. Years ago, business culture was relatively consistent. Today there can be enormous differences between companies, which may be exacerbated by mergers and acquisitions. We're working with many executives who are stuck in what William Bridges refers to in his book, *Transitions,* as "the neutral zone."[2] This is a place where someone has dis-identified with the old way of doing things but hasn't yet identified with the new way. It's a lonely place where people feel like they're failing to make transitions.

What's so difficult is that making the transition isn't simply a case of learning new skills. For instance, we often work with people who are moving from roles as individual contributors to ones in which they have significant management responsibility. Sometimes these people are unaware of the magnitude of this shift, or they may even be ambivalent about making the transition. In addition, they often struggle with shifts in value and philosophy. We work with professionals in the investment banking business, and many of them prefer to function autonomously. To expand their influence and compensation, however, they need to move into management roles. As part of our Action Coaching work with them, we help them focus on their mixed feelings about managing others and on how they feel about spending less time on what drew them to investment banking in the first place (having the freedom to

[2] Bridges, W., *Transitions* (Reading, Mass.: Addison-Wesley, 1980).

work their own way, having their work judged based on how much money they made for the firm, and so forth).

To help people make transitions, Action Coaching provides individuals with a forum in which to express their concerns and ambivalence. Action Coaching is also a way people can receive feedback about how they may be stumbling as they take transitional steps, and it's an intervention that clearly lays out the tangible and emotional roadblocks to making a given change and showing what people need to do to get past them.

Integrating Action Coaching into Your Culture

Anyone can benefit from the coaching lessons contained in this book. It doesn't matter whether your company is coaching-friendly or whether you want to coach peers, direct reports, or high-potentials. You don't need permission from your boss or formal approval from the head of HR to make this type of coaching work for you and your organization. Although certain qualities will make you a more effective Action Coach (qualities we'll delineate in a later chapter), you don't need any particular training or experience to implement this coaching process.

We write this, recognizing that you may work in an organization where there isn't a lot of internal coaching going on. Part of the problem is that coaching involves a substantial investment of time and energy in someone who may not respond to that coaching. Or someone may respond too well and be promoted out of the manager-coach's group. In addition, organizations don't always reward coaching — or at least they don't reward it in the way they reward other skills. The little coaching most managers do is on the fly. They offer good suggestions here and there, or they sit down once a year and offer a subordinate a detailed performance appraisal. What's missing is a consistent, formalized process.

About ten years ago at Honeywell, the company decided it wanted to encourage executive development on a managerial level; we recognized that development occurred through relationships that employees had with their managers. Honeywell set up awards for people who were superior developers of people, and they requested nominations for these awards. What is instructive is how everyone knew who these "developers" were. Everyone agreed that Don in marketing was terrific at coaching his people, that Mary in finance was brilliant at training her staff, and that Sam in human resources offered enormously insightful advice.

By example, you can become a quiet advocate of coaching in your organization. It's possible that management recognizes coaching's value but has no idea how to inculcate this competency throughout the company. Coaching is a soft skill that's difficult to measure, and management may be reluctant to institutionalize something that seems so fuzzy from both conceptual and implementation standpoints. Better to leave coaching to professional coaches is the usual thinking.

As professional coaches, we certainly can fill roles that insiders can't. At the same time, however, outside coaches can only do so much. A much better alternative is a combination of outside and inside coaches. For that combination to work, however, a process is needed that will meet individual and organizational objectives. A formal process reassures a company's leaders and gives them confidence that coaching is as much science as it is art. In the next chapter, you'll learn about the Action Coaching process and see how a variety of organizations have used it successfully.

2

The Eight Steps of Action Coaching

The Action Coaching process consists of the following eight steps:

1. Determine what needs to happen and in what context.

2. Establish trust and mutual expectations.

3. Contract with client for results.

4. Collect and communicate feedback.

5. Translate talk into action.

6. Support big steps.

7. Foster reflection about actions.

8. Evaluate individual and organizational progress.

This is a flexible process, in that you don't have to feel locked into the chronological order of the steps. In some instances you'll want to ask a client to reflect on his behaviors before the process starts, or you'll decide that it's clear what actions must be taken. Or you may have already taken some of the steps if you're coaching a direct report; you may be able to either skip steps or not spend as much time on them as if you had never worked with the person before.

You must, however, adhere to the four key elements of the process: (1) self-awareness is linked with business results; (2) an action plan is put in place; (3) the level of goal achievement is set based on organizational need; and (4) the process is structured and uses proven tools.

For instance, this means that you need to determine the goal level for your client—self-awareness, performance improvement, performance breakthrough, or transformation—based on what the company or the environment needs your client to do or become. If you leave this goal level open, your client may not change to the extent that the organization needs him to change, or he may change in ways that are unnecessary.

We hope this process overview will provide you with a sense of how Action Coaching unfolds and how you can implement it within your own organization; we offer tips and techniques that will assist you along the way. Although it's not a complicated process, it is one that requires skills and knowledge. Any process that attempts to reshape human behavior needs the hard-won expertise that we intend to share with you in this book. (See Exhibit 2.1 for a graphic representation of the process.)

Step 1

Even though it's important to identify new, desired behaviors, it's equally important to determine the larger context in which these behaviors need to happen. This makes it clear what the organization and the individual hope to get out of the coaching experience. When talking to your client about what you hope to accomplish, go beyond the problem (a behavior that is driving everyone crazy) or the developmental need (a high-potential who has to acquire a key skill). Help the person understand why this problem or need is of concern to the team, the department, and the organization. If you're a manager who is instituting your own coaching program, talk to your boss or someone else who has insight about the situation that is relevant to your coaching plans and share this insight with your client. Open up the discussion so that you understand the

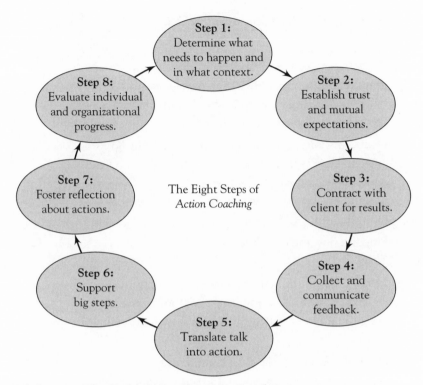

Exhibit 2.1. The Eight Steps of Action Coaching.

context—all the relevant factors and why and how the company wants an individual to change. Here's a checklist (Exhibit 2.2) you can use to start out in the right direction:

Context can also be shaped by significant organizational issues. You or someone else in the organization may want an individual to change in certain ways because of a company's new strategy or concerns about significant events (high turnover, a lack of organizational bench strength, and so forth). Here are four common corporate concerns that can be driving your coaching:

- *Succession planning.* In this instance, a company is reviewing talent and promotion possibilities when a coaching requirement is discovered. A potential successor is identified but it's determined

Exhibit 2.2. Opening Discussion Checklist.

Item	Completed
1. Move the discussion beyond the irritating behavior that's bothering you or the coaching candidate's boss; talk about the negative implications of that behavior on the team, department, company.	❏
2. Discuss organizational factors—the culture, the boss's attitude, direct reports' issues, competitive pressures, policies—that might be causing a particular behavior or stand in the way of the change you want someone to make.	❏
3. Pinpoint how the new skill will benefit the larger group.	❏
4. Identify how much of the change or development you require is based on your issues (or the sponsoring executive's issues) rather than on the organization's issues.	❏
5. Determine what goal level (self-awareness, performance improvement, and so on) is required for the person you are coaching.	❏

that despite his obvious assets in certain areas, he's missing a key ingredient—the ability to motivate people. Coaching is tailored to help the person develop this skill, with an organizational eye on filling a key position.

• *Organizational skill deficiency.* By this we mean that a company has uncovered a missing competency that is crucial to meeting strategic goals, and they need a number of key people coached so they can gain this competency. ARCO (now part of BPAmoco), for instance, recognizes that at some point in the future their employees will have to shift from managing domestic oil fields to managing fields in other countries. Managers will have to learn how to negotiate in foreign countries, work cross-culturally, and deal with other global issues. Although ARCO could send their leaders to some sort of global finishing school, they want more targeted interventions — targeted to the specific attitudes and behaviors of a given individual.

- *A specific problem or situation.* A high-potential person is messing up, and the organization wants to try and save her. It may be that this manager is on the brink of termination or is heading for the brink, and management has tried and failed to stop the slide. Action Coaching is a way to deal with the personal style issues, performance shortcomings, and motivational problems that are common in these situations. It is a way to handle delicate personal problems such as alcoholism and depression that may be contributing to the situation. Again, Action Coaching is counted on not just to "fix" the individual but to do so in a way that addresses organizational concerns about performance.

- *Transitions.* When new people are brought into an organization, promoted, or transferred to new jobs, a transition period takes place in which Action Coaching often proves useful. For instance, a new leader is recruited into an organization because of the need to "shake things up." The people who now find themselves reporting to the new leader may not agree that change is needed and may subtly resist the implied indictment of their own performance. The new leader will need to build allies while both adapting to a new culture and deciding what changes are needed. This presents a formidable challenge, which often results in the organism rejecting the transplant, and in the significant monies spent on recruiting, paying, and disengaging the new leader being wasted. Coaching during transitions can significantly reduce the risk of this happening.

The new president of Levi-Strauss sought coaching assistance to help him shape his agenda, his vision, and the team he inherited; he also needed to receive feedback. For the head of Levi-Strauss, Action Coaching was designed as one of a number of supports to facilitate his transition from one job to the next. Another common transition occurs when people are promoted and past behavioral histories are swept under the rug. Invariably, negative behaviors

Exhibit 2.3. Organizational Concerns That Drive Coaching.

Succession planning	A successor needs to develop certain skills before filling a key position.
An organizational skill deficiency	A crucial, strategic competency is missing companywide, so numerous people need development in that area.
A specific problem or situation	A key leader is having performance or personal problems.
Transitions	People move into new jobs that require new abilities.

from the past will resurface when a manager assumes a new role, and they usually will have more devastating consequences because the manager has more responsibility. Action Coaching is tailored to addressing these behavioral issues before they reappear and cause havoc. (See Exhibit 2.3.)

Step 2

The individual client's expectations may be different from those of the organization. Therefore, clarify what the purpose of coaching is, as well as what the client hopes to get out of it. Find out what the client's problem is and see how coaching can help her solve it. Does the individual understand the purpose of coaching? Does she feel she has a problem and, if so, what does she think it is? Does she need help in developing a new set of skills?

Give the individual a sense of what will happen during the coaching process. Sometimes we interview a variety of people — direct reports, customers, boss, peers. It's important for the client to understand that we'll be doing this so that he's not surprised when we start talking to people about him.

Initial meetings are also important for building rapport between client and coach. You can't force people to be coached. They need to enter into Action Coaching believing—or at least being open to the possibility—that the coaching process will help them meet their objective. During the first meeting or two, talk with your client about topics such as sources of satisfaction or dissatisfaction at work. Ask for a self-assessment of skills and competencies, explore your client's career and life aspirations, and in general attempt to create a degree of trust and compatibility.

The first meeting between coach and client often sets the tone for future interactions, and we'll explore how to handle this initial session in Chapter Six.

Step 3

This is a crucial step and one that is often missing from other types of coaching. Clients and coaches are held accountable for achieving specific, measurable goals that are stated in writing or orally. These agreed-upon outcomes often include one of the following:

Achieving a new level of performance (for example, in raising revenues, improving profitability, expanding market share)

Changing a customer relationship or improving customer satisfaction results

Improving scores on a survey of direct reports

Moving forward in one's career (for example, getting a promotion)

Improving relationships with one or more key people within the organization

Accomplishing a specific task (making a presentation, running a meeting, and so forth)

Achieving an organizational turnaround

Place the specific outcome within one of our four goal levels by asking yourself and your client these sorts of questions:

To accomplish a specific task, how much does this person need to change? Will it require just a bit of self-awareness or a major transformation?

To hit a performance target, will a performance improvement or a performance breakthrough be required?

To help this person further his career, just what types of new attitudes, behaviors, skills, and so on are required? To enable this person to be more committed to his work and find it more meaningful, what magnitude of change must be made?

As you're thinking about this goal level, keep organizational needs and factors in mind. Be forewarned that it's easy to become bogged down in an individual's behavioral issues and lose sight of the larger concerns. You'll get so caught up in a person's personality conflicts and anger at organizational policies, for instance, that you may start to focus only on resolving these conflicts or muting the client's anger. That's fine, but it may not be what will help the company improve business results or make a team more productive. To keep organizational issues in the forefront, you may want to have your boss or sponsor sign off on the contractual outcomes you establish before you go on to the next step.

Build some flexibility into these outcomes. Because they're established early in the process, neither the coach nor the client has the benefit of feedback that can better shape what the goals of the process should be. Although we often identify exactly the right outcome at the beginning, sometimes feedback causes both the coach and the client to rethink what the desired result should be. We may learn that problems in an area are more complex than we assumed and that a change in the client's behavior won't solve the problem—or that someone else will have to change their behavior (a boss, a direct report, a customer) for a solution to work. The point is that a certain degree of flexibility should be built into whatever outcome is in the contract between coach and client.

Step 4

To some extent, your coaching effectiveness will depend on your ability to gather and communicate feedback. Again, this may be new to you; it's not something most managers normally do. But if you want someone to make significant changes or achieve dramatic performance leaps, feedback will be a crucial catalyst. It's what moves coaching from a passive to an active experience; feedback motivates people to take action.

Assess how your client affects others, and communicate that impact to her. It's one thing for the client to give her own impression of her impact; it's something else entirely to obtain the impressions of her boss, direct reports, customers, and others. Collect these data through one-on-one interviews, surveys, and other means. The questions asked must be tailored to the specific outcome desired. For instance, if the desired goal is to develop more effective methods for managing people, then structure your questions around how well your client sets direction, recognizes contributions, and evaluates the performance of others. Although this isn't always true, a good rule of thumb is, *the more complex and ambitious the goal level, the more feedback that is required.* If an individual needs to transform herself, you're not going to motivate that transformation with vague and narrow feedback.

It may also be worthwhile for the coach to administer personal style or personality evaluation instruments to give clients a better understanding of their impact on others. These instruments include well-known ones such as the Myers-Briggs Type Indicator and newer ones such as the CDR Assessment and Leadership Risk Factors tool.[1]

[1] CDR Assessment Group (1998), Tulsa, Okla.

After gathering and evaluating all these data, provide feedback to clients. Even though you can rely on hard data from surveys and tests, integrate personal observations from your clients as well as the subjective impressions of others. In providing this feedback, keep the following issues in mind:

- What are the most important messages for the client?

- What does he need to hear?

- What information will most help him achieve his Action Coaching goals?

Communicating feedback to clients isn't simply a matter of telling them what was said. It's helping them deal with what they hear. It can be a shocking experience to discover that people perceive you differently from the way you perceive yourself. Let's say your coaching interviews reveal that, despite a client's best intentions to articulate his business strategy, other people don't understand it. Explain to your shocked client that the problem may be inadequate communication on his part, or it may be that other people are not sufficiently visionary to grasp his concepts. Whatever the problem, help your client understand that he has to make changes if he wants others to understand his strategy. Action Coaching almost always requires fact-based confrontation delivered in a provocative but caring manner.

Step 5

This is where you and your client determine what should be done — and when and how, based on the feedback the latter has received. Specifically, you should

Review and reset goals (if necessary); make sure that your goal level is appropriate and that it's connected to the business results your organization wants to achieve.

Explore different action paths to achieve these goals; discuss which ones seem feasible by identifying and evaluating the specific tasks as well as the possible obstacles each path entails; winnow the list of paths down to the one that makes the most sense from both the individual and organizational perspectives.

Identify the resources the chosen actions require (for example, financial support, training, job experiences, coordination with HR).

Set a time frame for achieving goals, keeping in mind when the organization needs your client to be up to speed and a realistic period for your client to change a behavior, develop a skill, and so on. As a general rule, self-awareness is a faster process than transformation.

Discuss the impact these achieved goals will have on the business and what measures will be used to assess this impact.

For instance, let's say that feedback reveals that a sales manager's customer base is too limited because he has problems dealing with customers who are different from himself; he's especially wary of dealing with companies in certain countries. The challenge here is to avoid assigning actions that are vague, lack accountability, or aren't linked to the appropriate goal level.

In this instance, you might agree that your client needs to set three appointments in the next month with companies in those countries he wants to avoid and report back on the results. This action, however, may yield nothing more than physical trips to uncomfortable places. Your client may report back that he now feels much more comfortable after the trips, but it may have nothing to do with his real feelings or, more important, the business results he generates. A more effective action plan would involve having the coach shadow the client on these trips and observe what happens. Or the plan should stipulate that the first step should be for the client to immerse himself in the culture of a given Third World country—that he needs to spend some time there, understand the customs, and learn more of the language before he even meets with a customer.

During this planning phase, it's important that coaches focus the work. We've found that after they receive feedback, some clients want to address each and every negative issue they hear about. To avoid this scattershot approach, you need to pinpoint the issues that will have the most impact on performance issues and limit objectives and actions to this select group.

Step 6

Action Coaching sends people out into the "field" to implement their plan. During this time, people need support from their coaches. For instance, Marcia was a high-potential executive who needed to learn how to become more trusting in order to develop into the leader the company required. In attempting to implement her action plan, which called for Marcia to give direct reports assignments and not question them every hour of every day, Marcia had serious qualms about what she was being asked to do. During our coaching sessions with her, we spent a great deal of time exploring what-if scenarios. Marcia needed to articulate these scenarios to us and reassure herself that nothing terrible would happen. Just being able to have people who weren't judging her listen to her admittedly paranoid fears helped her take the necessary actions.

Support can be as simple as lending an objective ear. It may involve regular meetings to monitor progress against the stated objectives. Or it may involve more intense sessions in which the client needs substantive advice in order to carry out the plan. You can assist your clients in all sorts of ways, from role-playing an interaction to providing information and insight. Support may mean you bring other people and resources in to help deal with an issue; it may mean you serve as a sounding board for an idea the client has; or it may involve helping the client work through difficult emotional issues.

This support function is crucial. To change long-held attitudes and behaviors, managers need different types of support. Change can be a scary process, and a coach's support can mean the difference between achieving a bit of self-awareness and making a performance breakthrough.

Step 7

One of the tenets of Action Coaching is that people need time to reflect on their attitudes and behaviors if they're going to change them successfully. Reflection, therefore, is built into the process. Have your clients stand back and look at their situations through your eyes as well as those of customers, peers, direct reports, and bosses. Encourage them and give them ways to reflect on what they're going through, why they're going through it, and what they're changing about themselves. You can facilitate reflection by asking the following questions (see Exhibit 2.4) or adapting them to specific situations.

Step 8

Assessment at the end of the process encompasses both hard and soft measures. In the former category are things such as customer outcomes, revenue increases, improved work conditions (for example, a faster turnaround time), increased efficiency or productivity, and so on. In the latter are measures such as how the client's group environment has changed, how satisfied the client was with the results of the coaching, how others around the client now perceive him. In some instances, we ask the same questions from the earlier feedback step of the same people months later and compare the responses.

Exhibit 2.4. Reflection Questions Checklist.

Question	Completed
1. Do you think you've changed in any way since you joined the organization?	❏
2. What is most troubling about the feedback you received? Why?	❏
3. If you could have done anything differently in the past, what would it have been?	❏
4. Why do you think the organization wants you to develop in this direction?	❏
5. Are there other doors to open that we've missed? Do you see alternatives to the actions we've decided on?	❏
6. What scares you the most about the ways we're asking you to change?	❏
7. In considering the behavior changes, skills to be developed, and other aspects of the action plan, what gets you the most excited about your career and your future with the organization?	❏
8. What have we intentionally not dealt with or incorporated?	❏
9. If we're sitting here a year from now, what might we expect to have happened?	❏

Ultimately, you're evaluating both whether the individual has changed his attitudes and behaviors and whether he's changed them along the lines that the organization hoped he'd change, as determined in Step 1 of the process. (See Exhibit 2.5 for a progress checklist.) As important as it is for the organization to see that progress has been made, it's just as important for the client. Once he recognizes that coaching has helped him make productive changes in the way he works, he's that much more likely to continue the progress he's made on his own.

Exhibit 2.5. Action Coaching Steps Checklist.

Step	Activity	Completed
1	**Determine what needs to happen and in what context.**	
	Determine type of coaching:	❏
	• Succession planning	❏
	• Organizational skill deficiency	❏
	• A specific problem or situation	❏
	• Transition	❏
	Conduct opening discussion (see checklist).	❏
2	**Establish trust and a set of mutual expectations.**	
	Determine how coaching will help the client.	❏
	Give client an overview of the coaching process.	❏
	Clarify mutual expectations.	❏
	Build trust (see Chapter Six).	❏
3	**Contract for results.**	
	Determine type of goal:	
	• Achieve a new level of performance.	❏
	• Change or improve a client relationship or results.	❏
	• Improve scores on a survey of direct reports.	❏
	• Move forward in career.	❏
	• Improve relationships with key organization members.	❏
	• Accomplish a specific task.	❏
4	**Collect and communicate feedback.**	
	Determine how the individual affects others:	
	• Interview "others."	❏
	• Administer instruments.	❏
	Deliver feedback to client:	
	• Identify most important messages.	❏
	• Identify what client needs to hear.	❏
	• Identify what information will most help client achieve his or her goals.	❏
	• Deliver feedback so client can hear it.	❏
5	**Translate talk into action.**	
	Set-reset goals at appropriate level.	❏
	Connect goals to organizational business results.	❏

(*continued on next page*)

Exhibit 2.5 (*continued*)

Step	Activity	Completed
	Explore different action paths, as well as specific tasks and obstacles.	❑
	Select action path with best fit for individual and organization. Identify resources needed.	❑
	Set a time frame.	❑
	Discuss the impact of goal achievement and how to measure it.	❑
6	**Support big steps.**	
	Meet or talk regularly to review progress on action plan.	❑
	Work through obstacles, fears, doubts.	❑
	Serve as sounding board.	❑
7	**Foster reflection about actions.**	
	Ask reflection questions (see checklist).	❑
8	**Evaluate individual and organizational progress:**	
	• How does the client think he or she has changed?	❑
	• How do others perceive the person has changed?	❑
	• How have the changes affected the organization?	❑
	• How satisfied is the client with the results?	❑
	• How satisfied is the organization with the results?	❑

Internal Roadblocks to the Process

You'll face certain obstacles when you try to obtain buy-in from the people you coach. As you might suspect, some people resist the premise behind any type of coaching. Many have had highly successful careers up to this point, and they refuse to acknowledge that they need help. Some people are also skeptical about Action Coaching's ability to produce tangible outcomes; they're doubtful that meetings with a coach can actually improve their business performance.

For the process to work, you need to shoot for at least a minimal level of self-awareness. Even if the stated goal falls in the performance improvement, breakthrough, or transformation categories, you need to start out with self-awareness as a base. This means you must help your clients acknowledge one of the following scenarios:

The behaviors and style that have helped them achieve so much in the past are no longer as effective; they need to accept that the environment has changed (or they're working differently); they need to realize that they have no choice but to change if they want to increase their effectiveness.

They have a blind spot when it comes to how they're perceived at work; they don't realize that certain behaviors inhibit their impact and effectiveness.

They're not performing at a sufficiently high level; they aren't achieving the goals demanded by their boss or by the job itself.

Most people are convinced that they're working as hard and as well as they can. They really don't think they can work harder, achieve certain goals, or change the way they manage and handle customers. Because they're defensive, have defined the situation incorrectly, or are in the dark for some other reason, they firmly believe that they can't (and sometimes shouldn't) change. You need to help them understand why and how they should change, and you can foster this self-awareness in many ways, including:

• *Confrontation*. Most managers don't like to confront; they prefer other, less direct and emotional ways of resolving problems. Coaches don't have this luxury. There are times when a coach has to be both direct and emotive to drive a point home. At times, only unambiguous, forcefully delivered facts prompt people to become deeply aware of what the real issue is.

• *Empathy*. There are also times when people need to talk to someone who really grasps what they're going through before they'll admit it to themselves. Active listening, making an effort to put yourself in someone else's position, and verbally communicating this fact will go a long way toward achieving self-awareness.

• *Higher purpose.* "It's not just about you in the here and now" is what you want your clients to understand. Lift them above the muck and mire of their daily struggles, and they begin to see the more important issues. Help them recognize how developing in a certain way will further their careers. Get them to understand that if they don't cease a counterproductive behavior, they will be letting their team down. Communicate that if they can achieve a performance breakthrough, the whole organization will benefit.

One of the premises of the Action Coaching process is that people can change their behaviors. We should add, however, that some behaviors are easier to change than others. If a manager, for example, needs to work on better methods for establishing goals and providing feedback to subordinates, that's easier than motivating her to do things that run counter to her personality and require transformation. Helping a by-the-numbers manager become more creative or a conservative executive become more decisive is difficult, and the process doesn't have a magic solution for these situations. Sometimes it can be a struggle, and it's important for both the coach and client to have patience and trust in the process (see Exhibit 2.6).

Process Variations

The process isn't always as linear as we've described. For instance, sometimes there isn't a clear end point and formal evaluation of outcomes. Some of our coaching relationships are ongoing, and they extend over months or even years, with informal evaluations of the coaching outcomes at points along the way. The focus of Action Coaching can also change, moving from one type of behavior or situation to another. We've started out working with a

Exhibit 2.6. The Client's Internal Roadblocks.

The Client's Internal Roadblocks	How to Overcome Them		
Formerly helpful behaviors no longer effective	**Confrontation**	⇨	Deliver information forcefully to make the person aware of the facts.
Blind spot about how he or she is perceived ⇨	**Empathy**	⇨	Listen, putting yourself in the person's position to encourage self-awareness.
Not performing at sufficiently high level	**Higher purpose**	⇨	Lift person above daily struggles to see more important issues at hand.

person on managing a difficult transition and moved to helping him with improving his performance during brainstorming sessions.

Another common variation is that the coach and client realize that other people need to be coached in order to achieve the desired outcomes. It may be that the individual can never become better at communicating what she wants her direct reports to do unless her direct reports become more adept at understanding what she requires. Or it may be that members of a client's team need an Action Coach to work with them; the client's behavioral changes will be meaningless unless key team members also change their behaviors. In instances when others are brought in to be coached, the process doesn't change so much as it widens; new substeps are added to the original eight-step process.

You also should be aware that the process can turn on a dime because Action Coaching is designed as a dynamic process. Let's say you're coaching a manager and as a result she gains insight into a performance problem. She realizes that both she and her boss have been misinterpreting organizational strategy and need to go back to the drawing board. Consequently, you may need to redefine your original desired outcomes and bring the manager's boss into the process.

It's also possible that you, the coach, can decide that the process isn't working and needs to be refocused. There have been times when we've realized we weren't doing a bit of good and stopped the process prematurely. There have been other times when it became clear to us that we needed to move in a new direction to be effective. For example, we started out working with the president of Levi-Strauss one on one, but after a period of time, we realized we could accomplish more if we worked with his group on some of the underlying issues.

Finally, the process can shift as the environment does. The company is merged or acquired; the higher-up executive who implemented the coaching process leaves the company; a new competitive thrust prioritizes a new competency (rather than the one for which someone was being coached). You need to be alert to these environmental shifts and try to move the process in the appropriate direction.

The Trick to Aligning Individual and Organizational Goals

This alignment is one of the most challenging aspects of the process. Before providing you with some Action Coaching strategies to meet this challenge, let's understand what you're up against when you try to coach an individual with larger organizational concerns in mind.

First, never forget that some people don't see the fit between who they are and what the organization is or what it wants to be. Every person we have ever coached saw his or her own behavior as rational and logical; it's the organization that's irrational and illogical. The challenge is to help people realize that their behaviors may be contributing to the organizational illogic and that if they are willing to try new behaviors, the organization may reflect the individual changes they've made. We had one client accusingly tell us, "You're trying to remake me, while I'm trying to remake the company!" We responded, "In the end, that's what will happen if we remake you first."

Second, the disconnect between individual and organizational goals is often due to an individual's motivation being at odds with organizational objectives. A coach we know told a team to share one good thing and one bad thing about working together at their regularly scheduled meeting. Things went fine for the first few meetings, but then team members began holding pre-meetings in which they made pacts, agreeing on what good things they'd say about each other and assuring each other that they would simply make the bad things up (so as not to hurt anyone's feelings). All of the team members were highly motivated — to preserve a good relationship with each other. Although they gave lip service to the organizational goal of improving open communication within the team, the individual goal of preserving relationships took precedence.

Third, coaches sometimes have problems addressing organizational issues. Traditionally, coaches are viewed as counselors for individuals, and organizational consultants are viewed as counselors for organizations. Never the twain shall meet. As part of the Action Coaching process, it's crucial to obtain buy-in from management to address both sides of the coin.

To link individual and organizational goals, coaches need to keep a close eye on individual motivation and make sure it fits with organizational strategy. If not, coaches need to find a way to motivate individuals so that it does fit. Keeping these goals in line requires collecting data from individuals both at the start of the process and as it unfolds. With organizational objectives in mind, coaches can assess the factors that are driving people in their work as well as the ones that are inhibiting them. The following questions are some that we use at the start of the process to assess these drivers and inhibitors:

What factors in the company influence your ability to perform your job?

What's pushing you to perform that job to the best of your ability? Compensation? Pride? Fear?

What is the overall direction and strategy for your organization, and do you agree with it?

What are your specific responsibilities? How clear are they and do they help or hinder your performance?

How would you describe your company's culture and how it affects your performance?

How would you rate the overall capacity of the people in your organization? Do they inspire you and pull together or discourage you and pull apart?

You certainly can structure your own questions along these lines. The key is to discover what pushes the individual toward organizational goals and what pulls him away from them.

Examples of the Process

We end this chapter with a few snapshots of Action Coaching programs, with an eye toward showing how the process addresses and coordinates individual and organizational goals. If you will be coaching people, this will be a primary concern for political as well as practical reasons. Coaching has traditionally been vulnerable to criticism that it has no impact on business strategy and results. We also know other coaches who have tried to make their work relevant to business objectives and failed. It's tough to link individual and organizational issues without a tried-and-true process.

The following three examples will give you a sense of how the Action Coaching process establishes this linkage:

Building Trust

A survey of two hundred managers at a Fortune 100 company revealed that they all distrusted the top management team. It was distressing to learn of this distrust in light of the company's goals: better synergy between different levels of the business, improved teamwork, and better group decision making. A typical coaching intervention might have been to work with individual members of this top team on their communication skills, their willingness to share responsibility, and so on. As Action Coaches, we started with the organizational goal of business synergy and examined how individual behavior contributed to or contradicted this goal. If we had simply helped a member of the team learn to open up to other managers, that may have improved communication but not synergy or teamwork; she may have become more open with others but remained unable to work productively and innovatively with them. Unlike other coaching interventions, Action Coaching always involves a litmus test of its effectiveness. At the end of the Action Coaching process here, another survey of these two hundred managers was taken to determine if the process had increased the trust level (it had).

Improving Client-Colleague Relationships

Arthur Andersen's Global 1000 Program involves partners who have global account responsibilities. The goal of this program is to help partners improve their client and colleague relationships. To that end, partners receive feedback from a variety of sources as well as the results of a personal style inventory and a work group assessment (climate inventory). As Action Coaches, we were called in to work with individuals who were part of this program and help them understand the messages contained in the feedback, put these messages in the context of the partners' current business challenges, and develop an action plan that would enable them to change attitudes and behaviors.

Although partners are encouraged to identify professional development goals as part of this Action Coaching process, they also must identify business targets (such as increasing revenue, expanding the customer base, or establishing a new practice area). The two are joined at the hip, and as coaches we make sure they stay joined throughout the process.

Adjusting to Company Culture

We were asked to work with a top executive at a larger corporation who was one of the few "outsiders" brought in at his level. The organization was concerned that this recruit was experiencing difficulty meeting his revenue targets and was taking too long to get up to speed. When we began coaching him, we learned that he felt that the culture was such that it was impossible to get anything done "unless you knew the right people." He simply wasn't used to working in a highly politicized, bureaucratic system and didn't know how to build alliances quickly. The Action Coaching process, therefore, accommodated two issues rather than the original one. Our data gathering and feedback helped this client realize that, although the culture was a problem, he needed to learn faster and build a network of allies and supporters in order to be more effective. At the same time, the feedback we received also corroborated this client's assertion that the culture was overly bureaucratic and political. We communicated to senior management that people often experienced culture shock when they joined the organization. Because the company was attempting to recruit other people for significant positions in the organization, this culture shock was a major concern. As a result, an orientation program for new hires was established.

We hope these examples give you a sense of the process and the unique way individual and organizational concerns are tied together. Although this process overview may give you a sense of *what* you might do as an Action Coach, you probably have numerous questions about *how* you get these things done. In the next chapter, you'll find a set of tools with which to carry out your ambitious mandates.

3

Action Coach's Toolkit

W e'd like to share some of our coaching tools with you. We can't share all of them because there are many tests, questions, and techniques that we rely on. Here you'll find the ones we think you're most likely to need when you're coaching, grouped according to each of our process steps. In most instances, we've singled out one key tool for each step, believing that if we can give you an understanding of a tool and how to use it, it will benefit you more than describing a wider variety of approaches in less depth. Some of these tools are original; others are modifications of existing tests and other instruments.

You'll find other tools and techniques scattered throughout the book, introduced when they're relevant to the subject at hand. Some are offshoots of the approaches introduced here; these demonstrate how you can use a tool in specific situations you're likely to encounter. The goal here, though, is to give you some practical devices that will make coaching a more manageable experience.

Determine What Needs to Happen and in What Context

What needs to happen is for your client to either change in ways that fit with the organizational context or to create a plan to change the organizational context. One of the biggest challenges for coaches is figuring out what this context entails. If you're a manager coaching a direct report, you probably have some sense of context. You know, for example, that the company is embracing diversity, and your direct report can only work with people who are exactly like he is. Many times, however, the organizational context is complex, changing, or multifaceted, and your take on it as a manager is limited to the work you do. There may be leadership development imperatives you're unaware of. Conversely, you may not recognize the underlying tensions caused by a new business direction.

In the previous chapter we described this step and some broad-brush actions you could take to identify organizational issues that relate to your client and to develop a plan that meets larger goals. Here we'd like to introduce you to our *organization-individual diagnostic*—a tool that provides more specific directions for accomplishing these goals.

The following diagnostic is flexible. Skip the questions you know the answers to, and rephrase questions so they fit your client's particular situation. The key with this tool is to gather information that helps you create a plan with organizational requirements in mind.

Gather Information

Start out gathering information from your client as well as others about what must be done for the organization (or department or team) to win. "Gain market share," "beat the competition," and "increase productivity" are three common responses for organizations. "Work more productively with others" and "develop a crucial new skill" are common responses for teams. You need to identify the most important factor for making the larger group successful. Ask the following questions:

What is the current agenda of the organization? What is the CEO emphasizing, and what are senior people being goaded on? What's the big strategic problem everyone is discussing?

What is happening in your environment—the industry, the company, the department, the team—that is affecting performance? Where are the opportunities to improve performance, and where are the roadblocks?

What are the customer, brand, or service issues that really matter to the organization? Have the programs designed to address these issues failed or succeeded? Why? Who should play a critical role in dealing with these issues?

What are the significant employee issues you're facing, including retention, employee loyalty, development, training? Are you losing the war for talent? Is it difficult to develop people quickly enough, to help them make significant changes, to create leadership?

We often use the Burke-Litwin Model of Organizational Performance and Change (Exhibit 3.1) to facilitate this analysis. Keep the following categories from this model in mind when you're investigating organizational issues: external environment, mission or strategy, leadership, culture, structure, systems, management practices, climate, and workforce capability.

Determine a Client's Stand on Issues

Once you determine what the key organizational or group issue is, focus your questions on where your client stands on this issue. Structure your questions on "feel-know-do" factors:

Do you *feel* like you've received fair recognition for your performance?

Do you *know* what is expected of you in this area?

What have you *done* to influence the results your group has achieved?

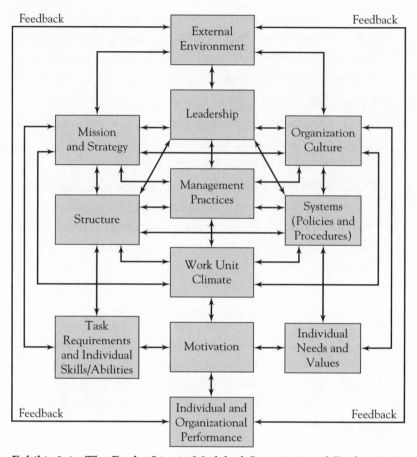

Exhibit 3.1. The Burke-Litwin Model of Organizational Performance and Change.

Source: Burke, W., and Litwin, G., "The Burke-Litwin Model," *The Journal of Management,* 1992, *18*(3). Reprinted with permission of *Journal of Management,* copyright © 1992.

Tailor these questions to the key issue. Let's say that a key requirement for a team is strategic thinking. Management needs this team to create more effective strategies that capitalize on available resources rather than strategies that are blue-sky thinking. Your questions might include the following:

Do you feel you've been properly trained to create the strategies the company requires?

Do you know the organizational strengths and weaknesses well enough to produce the strategies required?

What have you done to date in terms of strategic planning, and what have been the results?

You should also ask questions like this of others to ensure well-rounded feedback.

Develop a Plan

Determine what actions need to take place, based on the feedback received. In your assessment, consider the following factors before creating a plan:

Are the actions focused solely on your client, or must they involve others (direct reports, bosses, customers)?

Will there be resistance to the actions you're contemplating — the client finds it personally difficult to change, management support is lacking, the need to invest in training and development is urgent, the time frame is tight.

What are the benefits to the organization or group? Be specific about what the anticipated gain is, what the problem to be solved is, how performance is to be improved.

What are the benefits to the individual? How will these actions meet your client's personal agenda? Why will he be motivated to change?

Exhibit 3.2. Organization-Individual Diagnostic Tool.

Question	Completed

Organization Questions

1. What is the current agenda of the organization?   ❏
   What is the CEO emphasizing, and what are senior
   people being goaded on? What's the big strategic
   problem everyone is discussing?

2. What's happening in the environment — the industry,   ❏
   the company, the department, the team — that is
   affecting performance? Where are the opportunities to
   improve performance, and where are the roadblocks?

3. What are the customer-brand-service issues that really   ❏
   matter to the organization? Have programs designed to
   address these issues failed or succeeded? Why? Who
   should play a critical role in dealing with these issues?

4. What are the significant employee issues the company   ❏
   is facing, including retention, loyalty, development
   training? Is the company losing the war for talent? Is it
   difficult to develop people quickly enough, to help them
   make significant changes, to create leadership?

Individual Questions

1. Does the client feel that he or she has received fair   ❏
   recognition for performance?

2. Does the person know what is expected?   ❏

3. Does the person feel he or she has received adequate   ❏
   information and development to be successful?

4. What has the person done to achieve his or her goals?   ❏
   What have been the results?

5. Does the person know the organization well enough   ❏
   to be successful?

Action Questions

1. Are the actions required solely those of the client,   ❏
   or must they involve others (direct reports, bosses,
   customers, peers)?

2. Will there be resistance to the actions? (for example,   ❏
   the client finds it personally difficult to change;

Question	Completed

management support is lacking; there's a need to
invest in training; the time frame is tight)

3. What are the benefits to the organization or group?   ❏
What is the specific anticipated gain if the problem is
solved and performance is improved?

4. What are the benefits to the individual? How will   ❏
these actions meet his or her personal agenda? Why
will the person be motivated to change?

5. What is the goal level suggested by the actions (self-   ❏
awareness, performance improvement, performance
breakthrough, transformation)?

What is the goal level suggested by the actions: self-awareness, performance improvement, performance breakthrough, or transformation?

Establish Trust and a Mutual Set of Expectations

Although there are many ways to implement this step effectively, we use an approach we call *deep listening* that you should find useful. More than just a way to listen, it's a method for listening empathetically, objectively, and responsively. Here are the five components of the approach and instructions for using them:

• *Open-minded hearing.* When your client talks to you, silence the voice in your head that reflexively comments and judges. Focus all your attention on hearing. Suspend your internal monologue that is thinking about what to say next; be preoccupied with your client's words, not your own thoughts. When you listen intensely and without judgment, a bond is created with the talker. Your client will sense that she can trust you to be honest and fair.

• *Appreciative inquiry.* Reflect the other person's tone, feeling, and mood by restating the essential message. You can mirror what a client said or did with phrases such as, "So what you were trying to do in that situation was. . . ." or "What you seem to be saying is. . . ."

You can reflect a client's emotional state with phrases like, "So you were pretty frustrated at that point," or "That must have been tough on you." Appreciative inquiry is a way of offering support to a client; you're demonstrating that you appreciate what the person is going through and you're supporting the effort to deal with it. This not only builds trust but helps establish good communication.

- *Paraphrasing*. You're restating, not simply to let someone know you're listening but to move the discussion forward. Trust is built and expectations set when there is forward movement—when the discussion seems to be going somewhere. Paraphrasing encourages forward movement because it gives the speaker a chance to improve, correct, or add to what you've paraphrased. Preface your paraphrasing with "It seems to me that. . . ." to give your client an opening to correct your perception of things.

- *Confirmation of reality*. Communicate that you get what a client is saying. You're not necessarily agreeing, but you are demonstrating that the person's logic is understandable and that it's grounded in experience. Later on, you might have to help the client redefine her perception of reality. For now, you want her to feel that you empathize. Share a story that shows you've experienced this or a similar situation before. Or simply give the client a coherent explanation of what you think is going on inside of her and within the organization.

- *Self-disclosure and frankness*. You're a coach, not a therapist. Therefore, open up after listening. Share relevant problems from your past; talk about how you or someone else dealt with this type of issue. You want to be a warm rather than a cold listener, and this type of personal honesty will achieve that objective. As much as possible, talk about how you or someone else made the same types of changes the client is contemplating making. If the goal is a performance breakthrough, talk about someone who tried to make a similar breakthrough. Remember, however, not to shift the focus away from the client. The point of sharing your experience is to create a stronger bond between yourself and the person you are coaching.

Contract with Client for Results

This is when you get down to brass tacks. You're pushing your client to commit to a specific action and to be accountable for that commitment. Push often comes to shove, and this means you'll probably have to confront or challenge your client to secure a meaningful commitment.

We rely on a variety of confrontation and challenging techniques. Here are the ones that will be most useful to you:

• *Confrontation assessment.* As you're negotiating results, you should watch for certain red flags signaling that confrontation is necessary. Specifically, confront if your client:

Focuses only on her own growth and development and ignores the growth and development mandated by the organization or business requirements

Is only willing to make small-scale changes when larger ones are called for, for example, agrees to get feedback about her impact on others but refuses to commit to major performance improvement

Soft pedals the seriousness of a situation; insists that a problem is minor or that an issue will resolve itself

Denies an important piece of information that is obvious to everyone else

Blames others for the situation

Believes the situation or problem will blow over

Knows what needs to be done but is afraid to act or make a commitment to specific action

• *Concretizing reality.* This confrontation technique is useful for any of the red flags except the last one. Sometimes nothing you say will have anywhere near the impact that something you show will have. Provide your client with feedback from the CEO talking about how the company will never be the same as it was before the merger and its leaders need to change or get out. Offer tape-recorded evidence of problems that direct reports are having with your client. Take your client to an executive staff meeting and let him hear for himself about why new competencies are necessary.

• *Transfering ownership.* When you're talking with your client about what she might do and how she might change, you'll frequently hear something like, "Well, there's not much I can do since it's a systemic problem." People will blame systems, institutions, cultures, and karma for situations, thereby absolving themselves of responsibility for acting. You need to help the client take ownership of her problems. Challenge her excuses and rationalizations; don't allow her to get away with "Yes, but. . . ." statements. Try helping her take ownership of a problem by asking what she might do differently to change or have an impact on it — or what others might do. By demonstrating that she has options and that the problem is not insurmountable, the client is much more likely to own up to her role in creating the problem.

• *Connecting the dots.* Although direct confrontation that has an impact is necessary at times, coaches can also confront in a less dramatic, more conceptual manner. For instance, this technique involves helping clients see patterns by putting pieces of information together. Your client may have trouble recognizing other people's accomplishments and giving them feedback, but he attributes this to the culture. He tells you, "We don't celebrate much around here." You can confront him with the truth by showing him other pieces of information with the same message — a standardized test indicating that he's not very open or communicative or a number of performance reviews that suggest he could do a better job of encouraging his people. The cumulative weight of these individual pieces often motivates someone to make a meaningful commitment to achieve specific results. It's also useful if you want to demonstrate why the organization needs your client to change in specific ways—larger business goals sometimes require connecting the dots between strategies, an executive's or team leader's requests, and market requirements.

• *Stopping the action.* At some point during your conversation with a client, you'll find that he's exhibiting the same negative behavior in your interaction that is hampering him in the larger work environment. This is a great opportunity to call time out and point out what's happening right then. This can be eye-opening for people who, up to that point, haven't acknowledged or accepted a problematic behavior or attitude.

• *Call to action.* At some point, you need to ask your client, "What are you going to do about it?" After a certain amount of discussion and insight, you need to say something like, "Yes, I understand all the circumstances and reasons why you're in this situation, but what are you going to do?" With some resistant clients, you may have to pose this question with challenge, exasperation, and even the possibility of dire consequences. With others, you can ask it with curiosity and gentleness. Always, however, the message is that there's been enough talk and now it's time for action. This is also an appropriate time to move clients beyond the action of self-awareness to one of the other three goal levels.

Let us offer you one caution about using these confronting techniques. Sometimes you'll be delivering negative feedback, and it will be tough for the person you're coaching to acknowledge what you're saying. This is one reason we advocate building a trusting relationship in the previous step—it's much easier to accept negative feedback when you trust the person giving it. Be aware that you don't have to secure a commitment to specific results seconds after you confront. Some people need to mount a "self-esteem defense" before accepting the facts of a situation. Typically, they go through the stages of shock, anger, rejection, and acceptance. You should provide clients some leeway to vent these emotions. Let them make some excuses and react defensively for a bit before putting your foot down. (See Exhibit 3.3 for a summary.)

Exhibit 3.3. Confrontation and Challenge Tool.

Make confrontation assessment	Assess whether to confront by identifying red flags such as only making small changes, soft-pedaling serious issues, denying information, blaming, being noncommittal.
Concretize reality	Provide concrete evidence (record conversations, take client to a meeting to hear information, and so on).
Transfer ownership	When clients blame "the system," challenge their excuses and help them own their role and find options.
Connect the dots	Help clients see patterns by putting information together; use multiple pieces of evidence to build a case for change; link the change to larger business goals and benefits.
Stop the action	When the client exhibits the problem behavior with you, stop the interaction; call a time out to discuss what's happening.
Call to action	Stop the discussions and rationalizations and ask, "Yes, but what are you going to do about it?" to move from awareness to action.

Collect and Communicate Feedback

We provided you with guidelines on how to carry out this process step in the previous chapter. Because so much of feedback collection and communication is common sense, we'd rather focus on a tool that relates to feedback from tests you might administer to your clients. HR departments can advise you of the personality and other type of tests available, and you may have tests you know and like.

When you communicate the results of these tests to clients, however, you may be met with skepticism, disbelief, and absolute rejection, especially if the message is that performance breakthroughs or transformations are called for. To avoid or temper these reactions, consider using the tool shown in Exhibit 3.4.

Translate Talk into Action

One of the biggest challenges of coaching is to move clients from their verbal commitments to making changes in the way they lead, manage, and work. As much as people may want to change, they're not quite sure the form that change will take or how it might affect their careers, their workstyles, and their organizations. They often are concerned when you suggest that they need to achieve significant performance improvements or transformation. These are big leaps that are especially difficult to picture.

One way to translate talk into action is for clients to visualize their futures, and the tool shown in Exhibit 3.5 will help you in this regard.

The visioning-reframing tool consists of exercises and questions that give people the impetus to prioritize their activities in order to achieve a desired situation in the future. This is goal setting with the overlay of values. You want people to envision an ideal future for themselves, one in which they feel as if they're doing meaningful work. This provides powerful motivation to take action. To use this visioning-reframing tool, do the following:

Exhibit 3.4. Using Tests-Instruments Tool.

Action	Completed
1. Explain the purpose of the instrument and why you're using it in coaching.	❑
2. Describe what the instrument does and doesn't measure, how the results will be displayed, and conceptual frameworks used to organize the data.	❑
3. Describe any cautions (such as personality tests don't say much about ability or that people are often tempted to answer how they'd like to be rather than how they are).	❑
4. Before presenting results, give the client a chance to guess the scores. Most clients like doing this and it provides you a sense of their self-awareness.	❑
5. Describe the results. Pause for questions and check for understanding.	❑
6. Ask for reactions to the results. Is the person surprised? Watch for the common SARA reaction: shock, anger, rejection, and acceptance.	❑
7. Discuss the implications and how the results relate to the person's goals, the organizational requirements, and what the client needs to do to achieve them.	❑

• *Brainstorm.* Start out by asking your client to create a list of all the possible ways she might handle the current situation. Communicate that she should not feel restrained by current realities and that she should imagine all the ways she might change what she does, how she does it, and the various future scenarios that might result.

• *Create an ideal day.* You want to make the client's vision a bit more concrete here. Ask specific questions about what she would be doing on an ideal day, what position and role she would be in, who she would be meeting with, and what projects they would be working on. It often helps to have people write out their ideal day; this exercise lends itself to creative writing. Then discuss

Exhibit 3.5. Visioning-Reframing Tool.

Brainstorm	Create a list of possibilities, unrestrained by current realities; imagine a variety of future scenarios.
Create an ideal day	Make the vision more concrete by imagining specific occurrences of an ideal day; have the person write this out.
Write a magazine story	Have the client create a story, three years out, that features their situation on the cover of a business magazine; an example: "The Best Managed Company in the World."
Anchor the vision in reality	Ask questions to make the vision more real; ask about work the person would be doing, their impact on the organization, similarities or differences to the current situation, and so on.

the ideal day and analyze what needs to take place for this ideal to be realized.

• *Write a business magazine cover story.* Assign the client a story with the headline, "The Best-Managed Company in the World" (or best-managed team or best-managed department). Say that the date of the story is three years hence and that the story should be brief; it should explain why the client's company (or other group) is the most admired in the world. Again, discuss the story and have the client talk about how his vision for the group relates (or doesn't relate) to the vision he has for himself.

• *Anchor the vision in reality.* Move from the ideal to the real by asking people a series of questions that look to the future clearly and directly. The purpose of these questions is to elicit specific ideas about what they and their groups or companies will be like a few years from now. Some questions you can use to this end are

In what type of work will you be engaged three years from now?

What impact will you be having on your organization?

What type of success will your company be enjoying?

What role will you play in this success?

What are the similarities and differences between your current role and the role you'll play in the future?

How will your self-awareness, performance improvement, performance breakthrough, or transformation affect direct reports, peers, bosses, customers, your team, your department, your company?

Support Big Steps

Role-playing is a terrific tool to support the actions your client needs to take. When the action involves a significant change in behavior or attitude or requires a performance improvement or breakthrough, dress rehearsals are important. You'll find that it gives your client a chance to test the waters and see how a new behavior or way of conducting business feels. Although there are many approaches to role-playing, here's the one we've found to be most effective within a coaching framework.

One general piece of advice about this tool: don't let the role-play scenarios go on too long. A minute or even thirty seconds often suffices. Get in and out of the roles quickly, and then talk about them. Now let's look at how role-playing unfolds (see Exhibit 3.6).

You might also consider the following role-play variations to provide support:

• *Reverse roles.* You pretend to be your client and have your client be the other individual in the scenario. This helps the client see things from the other person's frame of reference and allows him to see himself more objectively. This requires a bit of acting ability on your part, but you know your client pretty well by this point so it's not such a difficult task.

Exhibit 3.6. Role-Playing Tool.

Action	Completed
1. Identify the specific action that needs to be taken and the context in which it will occur (a meeting, presentation, and so on).	❑
2. Discuss the situation and determine who will be involved, the different "players" perspectives on the issues involved, the relationships between the players, expectations and attitudes of those involved.	❑
3. Talk about whether there are any hidden agendas.	❑
4. Ask what the client's ideal outcome will be and his or her worst fears.	❑
5. Conduct the role play. Have the client play him- or herself, and you play the other key person.	❑
6. Debrief the role play. Discuss how it went, what went well, what might have been done differently, what was learned.	❑
7. Provide the client with feedback and suggestions based on the exercise.	❑
8. Establish a plan for moving forward in similar situations.	❑

Optional variations
- Reverse roles: You be the client, he or she is the other key player.
- Create worst-case scenarios and act them out.
- Videotape the role play and review it for additional learning.

- *Create worst-case scenarios.* Set up the situation so that your client's worst fears are enacted. If the situation involves your client asking a boss for more resources, turn him down cold. If it has to do with your client confronting a direct report with a difficult truth, break down crying when you hear it. Rehearsing disasters and extreme situations takes some of the fear out of taking a given action.

- *Videotape the role-play and then view it with your client.* Stop it at key points and ask: What was going through your mind then? What were you trying to accomplish? What's wrong with this picture?

Foster Reflection About an Action

The tool and the process step are the same here (see Exhibit 3.7). If there is any one skill that action coaches need, it's the ability to foster reflection in their clients. *Reflection* is a way for your client to make sense of the actions she needs to take, and once they make sense, they're that much easier to act on. It's impossible for her to transform herself without reflection; even self-awareness requires a considerable amount of reflection.

Reflection is catalyzed in many ways, and you will probably need to experiment with the following techniques to see which ones work with your clients:

- *Encourage thinking about what's really important and meaningful.* Prompt clients to consider what they truly value in life and how their work might become value-consistent. Thinking about what's meaningful and how to achieve it can secure a commitment to a given action.

- *Have clients focus on obstacles and resistance.* The idea here isn't to create strategies to overcome obstacles as much as it is to realize that things will need to be done differently. When people contemplate what stands between them and their goals, they start challenging their own beliefs and assumptions, and this leads to personal change and performance gains.

- *Suggest that clients rewrite the script.* In other words, have them think about what it would be like if things were different. If

Exhibit 3.7. Reflection Tool.

Values check	Encourage thinking about what's really important and meaningful in work and life; determine what the client values most.
Obstacles review	Focus on what stands between the person and his or her goals to increase motivation.
Script rewrite	Have the person reflect on "what it would be like if" an opposite or foreign reality were not only possible but happening.
Key learnings	Ask the person to review what he or she has learned in the coaching process so far.
Ask three questions	Have clients ask themselves three questions: What's happening? What's not happening? What can I do to influence the action?
Reflect	Encourage reflection on key assumptions.
Keep journal	Suggest clients keep a regular journal outlining feelings and ideas.

they feel powerless now, what would it be like to feel powerful? You're often asking people to reflect on an opposite reality—or at least one that feels foreign—and this gets them thinking in new directions.

• *Ask clients to reflect on key learning*—to consider what they've learned from the coaching process so far. How would they act differently in a key situation? What skills do they need? What do they have to do to take advantage of opportunities?

• *Use the Vietnam model.* General Gordon Sullivan tells a story about how commanders in Vietnam learned to ask three key questions in the midst of battle in order to work through their anxiety and decide what to do next: What is happening? What is not happening? What can I do to influence the action? Reflecting on these questions will help your clients act rather than be paralyzed by anxiety and indecision.

- *Push clients to reflect on key assumptions.* What often prevents people from taking the actions planned in the coaching process is their assumptions. Many times they don't make necessary changes or develop in key ways because they *assume* that it really won't help the team or business. For example, a client refuses to raise outside-the-box questions during team meetings because he's convinced that they won't really benefit the team or that team members will reject them and view him as a lightweight. Get him to reflect on this assumption by using the "When you do (or don't do) this, you seem to believe that. . . ." opening. For instance, "When you consider proposing an unusual idea to your team, you don't do it because you seem to believe the team is inherently conservative and judgmental. What do you think about that?"

- *Have clients keep a journal containing daily or weekly reactions, feelings, and ideas.* Suggest they e-mail journal entries to you and tell them you'll give them feedback. Another way you can structure the journaling process is by asking them to write about their coaching goals and planned actions: Did they take any of these actions today? How did they feel when they tried to do what was agreed upon? What did they learn?

Evaluate Individual and Organizational Progress

The evaluation tool you use should be based on the coaching plan and goals established earlier in the process. Performance reviews, 360-degree feedback, management team review of productivity increases, and other devices are all appropriate. Whatever approach you choose, you will find the tool shown in Exhibit 3.8 helpful for charting progress.

All these tools will help you balance the individual needs and issues of your client with larger business requirements (see Exhibit 3.9 for a summary). Although experience is the best way for you to maintain this balance in your coaching, the next chapter will provide some useful tips and information.

Exhibit 3.8. Evaluation Tool.

Action	Completed
1. Has your client achieved the targeted goal?	❏
2. What specific changes in behavior and attitude indicate that this goal level has been reached?	❏
3. If you believe the goal has been reached, specify why these changes are sufficient to meet the criteria of the goal level.	❏
4. Does the client feel the goal has been reached? Does this achievement help meet his or her job and career objectives?	❏
5. How does the client believe job and career objectives have been met?	❏
6. What motivated the person to achieve these objectives? Will this motivation continue to keep the person on track?	❏
7. Do others in the organization (boss, HR, peers, direct reports, customers) believe the client has met key organizational requirements?	❏
8. How do they describe the changes showing that the requirements have been met?	❏
9. If the requirements have not been met, where do they believe the client has gone off track?	❏

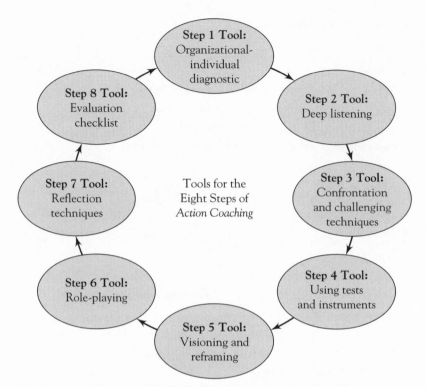

Exhibit 3.9. Tools for the Eight Steps of Action Coaching.

Part II

The Coach's Edge

*Linking Individual Motivation
and Company Performance*

4

How to Coach for Individual and Company Performance

As helpful as the tools and process of the previous chapters might be, they are no substitute for experience. Although many of you may have coached direct reports, peers, and others informally, you probably haven't considered coaching an integral part of your job. Even if you have done some coaching, the odds are that you went about it in a traditional way. Consequently, you may not have a backlog of experiences to turn to when you run into the roadblocks and complexities that are part of most coaching situations.

This chapter is no substitute for experience, but it can help you learn to think like an Action Coach. Specifically, the following questions need to be asked routinely when you start coaching: What behavior is my client exhibiting? What impact is it having on others? What do we know about it? How is this behavior linked to an organizational or business requirement?

The more familiar you become with common behaviors and business requirements—and the various intersections between the two—the more effective you'll be as a coach. In this chapter we discuss fourteen types of behaviors that create problems. They aren't the only problematic behaviors, but they're the ones you're most likely to encounter. Similarly, we describe seven common business requirements that can require coaching. Again, they are not the only ones, but they recur time and again.

Even if you find yourself dealing with a behavior or business requirement that is different from the ones we discuss here, this chapter will stand you in good stead. The natural tendency of most managers is to focus exclusively on the behavior that's causing problems or the business results or requirements that you feel pressure to meet; these must be given equal weight. Keep in mind that coaching requires you to reframe your perspective by including both behavioral and business requirements.

Types of People Who Exhibit Unproductive Behaviors

Your first experience using the process described in this book probably will occur because a boss tells you to work with someone with a problem or because you decide on your own that a peer or direct report needs help. Although it's possible that the catalyst for coaching is a development need—a high-potential requires your guidance to acquire a crucial skill—it's more likely to be a behavioral issue.

We think it is useful to recognize fourteen of the most common types of behaviors that produce a call for coaching. They also reflect the dimensions of a new tool we use extensively called the CDR Leadership Risk Profile[1] that enumerates the ways in which executives derail. The executive is provided with a comprehensive summary of potentially "risky" behaviors engaged in during periods of stress, along with developmental suggestions for curtailing these excesses. Keeping an eye out for these familiar categories, understanding what lies behind these behaviors, and seeing how they derail careers and thwart performance will assist you in your coaching. We're indebted to Morgan McCall and Mike Lombardo of the Center for Creative Leadership in Greensboro, N.C., for their pioneering work on career derailers.[2]

---

[1]CDR Assessment Group (1998), CDR Leadership Risk Assessment, Tulsa, Okla.: Author. (source for the following scale names: Egotist, Cynic, Loner, Hyper-Moody, Pleaser, Worrier, Upstager, Perfectionist, False Advocate, Rule Breaker)

[2]McCall, M., and Lombardo, M., *Off the Track: Why and How Successful Executives Get Derailed* (Greensboro, N.C.: Center for Creative Leadership, 1983).

As you begin interviewing and gathering data about the people you're coaching, keep an eye out for the following behavioral types.

The Bully

People who use bullying behaviors are unfairly capitalizing on their positional authority by abusing those around them. They don't simply shout and belittle (though these are certainly ways bullying can manifest itself); they may impose unrealistic demands or withhold recognition. It may be that they've been effective in their job for a while (usually because they do everything themselves) but they become less effective over time. People who work for bullies become alienated; "weak" people end up with the goal of avoiding abuse and strong people end up leaving.

Coaching Tips

- Determine whether bullying is widespread or limited to one type of situation; transformation may not be necessary if bullying is a "limited" trait. All that may be necessary is self-awareness.
- Assess whether bullying has a negative or positive impact on performance; what someone may consider bullying may actually be a response to a critical situation, and the bullying is nothing more than your client pushing hard to reach an important goal or acting as a change agent to drive for results.

The Egotist

Self-centered and self-aggrandizing, this type of person communicates to others a sense of entitlement. Egotists overvalue their capabilities and are often shocked to discover that others don't value all the things they do. They also have trouble accepting other people's points of view, preferring their own. They come across as arrogant to people around them. Egotists often make others uncomfortable, but they rarely notice the discomfort they cause. Every manager and leader requires a healthy ego, but when that ego is out of control, people become blind to their own shortcomings, fail to recognize and respond to the needs of others, and miscalculate important trends (because they only listen to what their ego tells them and don't take in perceptive observations from others).

Coaching Tips

• Determine whether the behavior issue is a direct result of a new organizational emphasis on teams; egotists often have trouble making this shift, and awareness of the problem might be all that's required. Some egotists are merely fearful, possibly of not getting credit or of losing the career race, and overcompensate.

• Use feedback, shadowing, and other tools to ascertain whether a person's ego makes him or her blind to larger issues; egotists, no matter how talented they might be, cause serious problems when they fail to see how others might contribute to dealing with a situation and how some factors are beyond their control.

The Cynic

Micromanaging is a trait of cynics. You should be aware that cynics' behavior goes beyond making snide or caustic remarks now and then; they have difficulty trusting others. This inherent distrust makes them poor delegators and team players. By rarely uttering an optimistic or positive word, they demoralize those who work with them. You may also discover in collecting feedback that people who work for cynics have difficulty learning and developing; cynicism discourages anyone from taking chances, trying new things, and learning from these experiences.

Coaching Tip

• Differentiate between healthy skepticism and demoralizing cynicism. If your client is in a position of authority, and feedback tells you that her attitude is robbing the people who work for her of initiative and inspiration, you should point out how this behavior is having an impact on business goals. Cynicism is often the marker for extremely frustrated idealism—another path for the coach to explore.

The Loner

Some of the common words you'll hear to describe this type of person are *uninvolved*, *unaware*, and *isolated*. Such people may be cerebral leaders who come up with brilliant strategies in their ivory towers, but they're terrible at communicating these strategies. For years organizations tolerated productive loners—people who were allowed to be lone wolves and operate on their own as long as they did their job. In a team environment, however, loners are difficult to tolerate, especially if they're in managerial positions. Detached, indifferent-seeming managers generally don't take into account the needs and goals of direct reports; they're very poor motivators. Poor at reading organizational politics and not particularly good at establishing visibility for their team or group, loners tend to have little impact.

We worked with an executive who exhibited many of these loner behaviors. He usually preferred concentrating on technical issues by himself in his office rather than drawing on his group's expertise. In fact, he only seemed capable of communicating with others one on one; he was awkward in any group situation. His team, needless to say, did not have many meetings. Because of this, he was not aware of problems until they reached the crisis stage. Rather than use meetings as a forum for people to air issues and determine whether a situation needs to be addressed, he relied on conversations with one or two people and never saw the big picture.

Coaching Tip

- Here is the key question for you to answer: For the loner to do her job effectively, does she need to interact well with others, motivate, and provide clear and constant direction? If not, the loner behavior may not be difficult for you to resolve. All that may be required is a little moderation in that behavior. Some jobs don't require a high level of skill in interacting with others.

The Hyper-Moody

We're using this term to describe people who are emotionally inconsistent. Their mood swings make it difficult if not impossible for people to work with them effectively. One day they may be highly enthusiastic about a project, and the next they may be indifferent to it. Volatility is another trait that suggests this type of person. If you hear stories about people who become inappropriately angry when a problem arises and then react with indifference when that same problem occurs again, you are probably dealing with a hyper-moody manager.

A few years back, we worked with Shelly, an executive who could be extremely pleasant and engaging one moment and brutally critical the next. She might rally her group around a project and inspire them to work themselves nearly to death for a week and then lose interest, causing her people to wonder why they had worked so hard and to vow they'd never do it again.

Coaching Tip

- Listen for feedback such as "We never know where we stand with her" and "People always ask his secretary what mood he's in today." These are giveaways that you're dealing with this type of client.

Figure out whether your client is in denial about this behavior. If he claims that "everyone gets in a bad mood now and then," yet the evidence is that his wild mood swings are alienating and egregious, then the problem may require intensive work to get at the root of it.

The Pleaser

You've probably seen this behavioral type surface when people are promoted and given more responsibility. Suddenly they become timid and unwilling to challenge authority; they're eager to please and often indecisive. Pleasers are often unable to take the risks necessary in modern, changing organizations. Because they want to hold on to their new authority at all costs or for other reasons, they become cautious at best and sycophantic at worst.

A common behavioral manifestation is a failure to support one's people. Mandy, for instance, was attending a presentation that some of her people were making to a senior leadership group. When the presentation didn't go well, Mandy was quick to criticize. Not only did this upward-serving behavior alienate the people who worked for her but the other senior executives disapproved of the way she had failed to support her direct reports.

Coaching Tip

- Analyze whether risk taking is important for the person you're coaching from the organization's perspective; to accomplish her goals, does she need to take risks consistently?

This behavior may be a temporary result of any one of many factors — a promotion, some upheaval in her personal life, and so on. So evaluate whether this behavior is relatively new and might self-correct on its own.

The Worrier

Some people doubt their own abilities and have a deep fear of criticism and of making mistakes. They can be labeled as predictable, or conservative. Some identifying remarks about this type of person are, "He's never willing to try anything new" and "She's done everything the same way for the last five years." At a time when organizations require managers and leaders to recognize the importance of continuous learning, worriers can cause serious problems. When they resist changes or fail to try new methods and techniques, they roadblock all sorts of initiatives. People who don't constantly examine their own assumptions in light of new information often fall into this category.

"We've tried that before and it didn't work" is another common remark that worriers make when someone suggests a new approach. In fact, we worked with one executive who said exactly these words when an acquisition was proposed that would have expanded the company's market presence in an important region. Although he was right—the company had tried this type of acquisition and it hadn't worked out—that was over ten years ago. This executive refused to factor in all the changes in the marketplace and other emerging issues that mandated keeping an open mind about an acquisition. He was worried about taking a chance.

Coaching Tip

- Discover whether your client is mirroring the attitudes of the company's culture, his boss, or a previous employer; the cause of his worries may be rooted there.

- Find out what your client is afraid of (fear often mires people in tradition); talking about that fear and creating an action plan to deal with it may result in a performance improvement.

The Upstager

Some people need to be the center of attention and are unable to share credit. They can also give the impression that they're much more capable than they really are; they may have one special skill but are deficient in others and adept at hiding this deficiency. Upstagers often make a big splash at a particular job and set expectations higher than they should be. Sometimes this isn't their fault. We see this with high-potential executives moved quickly through development assignments on their way to bigger and better things. Because they're not given sufficient time to allow their flaws to surface, they seem golden. Although they can get away with thriving on one or two superior skills for a period of time, eventually it catches up with them.

Julia, a telecommunications company executive, enjoyed a reputation as a big-picture thinker in an organization filled with short-term plodders. Given plum developmental assignments, she was quickly promoted and became the first woman in the company's history to be named an officer before the age of forty. She craved attention, but as she gained greater visibility and responsibility, her flaws were exposed. Her ideas were still good, but she failed to roll them out in ways that delivered results. Her inability to share credit alienated her peers and direct reports. She developed a reputation for selfishness that pushed away all the good people she needed if she were to achieve great business results.

Coaching Tip

- Upstagers often are great candidates for developmental action plans. You need to help them become aware of their flaws and motivate them to gain the competencies the organization deems necessary for their position and teach them how to generate loyalty and commitment from the people around them. This can result in significant performance improvement or breakthroughs.

The Transition-Challenged

On the surface, it may seem that people like this were bad hires or should never have been transferred to a new position. It's easy to jump to the conclusion that someone simply wasn't cut out for a particular company or the demands of a given position. In fact, the problem may be that the person is not adept at transitions and his or her behaviors reflect this problem. John Gabarro of the Harvard Business School has studied managerial transitions and found that those who did well were able to create mutual expectations regarding performance and roles, establish trust through integrity and openness, and use personal influence rather than positional authority to get things done.[2] When people begin jobs at organizations with strong cultures, transition problems are exacerbated.

[2] Gabarro, J., *The Dynamics of Taking Charge* (Cambridge, Mass.: Harvard University Press, 1987).

Sometimes the problem behaviors are a result of the transition rather than an inherent inability to perform a job.

Coaching Tip

• Answer these questions early on: How big a transition is your client being asked to make? Does your company have a strong (or unique) culture that many new hires have difficulty with? Has your client had trouble with other transitions in the past? What you're attempting to discover is whether this behavior is deep-rooted or a result of surface issues.

The Small-Picture Thinker

The odds are that you'll encounter some managers who are experiencing major career problems because they are uncomfortable thinking in strategic terms or taking significant risks. They prefer focusing on technical or tactical matters, but at some point they're promoted to positions in which they need to demonstrate big-picture thinking. As an Action Coach, it's important to determine whether their failures as strategists are due to lack of skill in this area or simply discomfort with applying what they know how to do.

As one of her bank's top traders in the bond market, Jennifer was given her own business to run. Virtually overnight she went from working alone to managing a large group of people. As you might expect, she maintained her "producer" mind-set as a manager, failing to map out a strategy or come up with a vision for her business. Her instinct was to fall back on her technical strength when the business faltered rather than to develop her weakness. As a result, she stubbornly used tactics when she needed a strategy.

Coaching Tip

• Recognize that not everyone is a visionary or big-picture thinker. Find out how difficult it really is for your client to think strategically, to create a vision of the future. Does your client not know what's required, or is she unable to do what needs to be done?

The Team Wrecker

Sometimes we encounter managers who have been placed in leadership positions but run into problems because they surround themselves with the wrong people. The managers themselves may be visionaries and great strategists, but they build a staff or team that is unbalanced or ill-suited for the job. These executives sometimes (consciously or not) hire people who don't pose a threat—they aren't so technically skilled that their talents surpass the leader of the group, and they aren't so aggressive that they're likely to challenge his authority. As a result, the group doesn't perform well. In other instances, team wreckers choose the right people but can't help them clarify their roles and responsibilities or develop trusting relationships. And some simply don't read the organization properly and fail to select team members who will help achieve what the organization wants them to achieve.

Coaching Tips

- You need to determine what's causing these leaders to create a group or staff that is lacking in some critical way. Reflection may be a good tool to use to help your client contemplate why her teams always seem to perform poorly; straight analysis might not yield the answer, especially if she's a true team wrecker.

It may be worth considering whether your client really should have a team leadership role; you should communicate with someone in management about other roles for which this person is better suited.

The Perfectionist

Details are important, but you may find yourself coaching someone who is so fanatical about details that it's standing in his way of moving to the next level. Many managers have been raised in cultures where precision and "covering all the bases" have been emphasized, so it's not surprising that some of these people become carried away with rules and procedures. Perfectionists are often inflexible and obsessive about doing things in a certain way. They drive their people crazy, which results in numerous complaints that cause Action Coaches to enter the picture. At their worst, perfectionists will look at a brilliant forty-page report slaved over by their direct reports and obsess about the typos. Sometimes, an entire company can be populated by this type of person, striving for perfection and demanding it of others. These companies must actively promote the "80 percent" (perfect) solution as acceptable.

Coaching Tip

• Determine whether this irritating behavior is connected to other, more serious problems. Perfectionists might be so obsessive about little things that they overlook big strategic factors, or they might be extremely narrow-minded and ignore valuable input. They might also be responding to the demands of the corporate culture. If these other, more serious problems are involved, it's likely that they're big roadblocks to performance.

The False Advocate

We've coached a number of people who have sabotaged their careers and their performance through behaviors that a psychologist might term passive-aggressive. We prefer the term *false advocate*. Most organizations have some managers who exhibit this maddening behavior. They sit in meetings and nod or say nothing when a decision is being made, appearing to accept the decision. Afterward, they ignore the decision and do as they please. Or false advocates might simply disregard requests people make, never explaining why they're disregarding them or saying they don't want to do something. In other words, disagreement surfaces covertly rather than overtly. The problem, of course, is that false advocates undermine projects by seeming to give a buy-in and then acting as if they're dead-set against it.

Coaching Tip

- Explore what false advocates are angry about. Anger often fuels this behavior, and if you help the individual you're coaching to surface and talk about his anger, you may start him on the path to moderating his behavior.

The Rule Breaker

These people are tough to manage and tough to coach. They can be exciting to be around because they constantly challenge "the way we do things around here." The problem is that they want to break rules just for the sake of breaking them. They are constantly pushing the boundaries and have little tolerance for people in authority. They act impulsively, sometimes without thinking about consequences. Although they often have terrific social skills, they can get bored easily and move on to something else, whether or not everyone else is ready to join them.

Coaching Tip

- Help rule breakers understand their impact. Because of their social skills, they have good relationships with other people in the organization. Get feedback on how their behavior affects others.

Point out the consequences of their behavior on the organization; help them learn the difference between finding new ways to do things that are important to the business and doing things just to be different.

See Exhibit 4.1 for a checklist to use when evaluating a client's behaviors.

Exhibit 4.1. Unproductive Behaviors Checklist.

Would you characterize your client as doing the following?	Yes	No
1. Unfairly capitalizes on his or her positional authority to abuse people? **(Bully)**	❑	❑
2. Overvalues his or her capabilities, has trouble accepting others' views, comes across as arrogant? **(Egotist)**	❑	❑
3. Distrusts others, micromanages, delegates poorly? **(Cynic)**	❑	❑
4. Operates alone and communicates strategies poorly; an isolated, often cerebral strategist or technical specialist? **(Loner)**	❑	❑
5. Is enthusiastic one day and indifferent the next? Volatile? **(Hyper-moody)**	❑	❑
6. Is eager to please and unwilling to challenge authority to support his or her people? **(Pleaser)**	❑	❑
7. Is unwilling to try new things or keep up with changing trends? Often says, "We tried that and it didn't work"? **(Worrier)**	❑	❑
8. Gives the impression of being more capable than he or she is; stellar in one skill but deficient in others? **(Upstager)**	❑	❑
9. Is not adept at making transitions; seems like a bad hire? **(Transition-challenged)**	❑	❑
10. Is uncomfortable thinking in strategic terms? Focuses on technical details? **(Small-picture thinker)**	❑	❑
11. Builds a staff or team that is unbalanced or ill-suited for the job? Hires weaker people? Fails to motivate the team? **(Team wrecker)**	❑	❑
12. Obsesses about details, "covers all the bases," is carried away with rules and procedures and inflexible? **(Perfectionist)**	❑	❑
13. Appears to support decisions (or say nothing) and then does what suits afterward? Disregards requests with no explanation? **(False advocate)**	❑	❑
14. Constantly breaks rules just for the sake of breaking them? **(Rule breaker)**	❑	❑

Types of Organizational-Business Requirements

In Chapter Two, we talked about broad organizational goals for coaching, such as helping people acquire critical skills or developing into more effective leaders and managers. As a coach, these broad mandates aren't particularly useful from an evaluation and action planning standpoint. You need to make these mandates more specific. If you've been assigned coaching responsibility, you might need to talk more with the sponsor about what the company wants from an individual. If you're coaching a peer or direct report, you may still need to talk to someone in management or in HR to pinpoint how the company, division, or team might benefit.

In the sections to follow, we'll describe seven common business requirements. The list of requirements is not inclusive, but it does contain common requirements that you'll probably run into. As you read about these requirements, you'll see that we're constantly referring back to our behavioral types. This is the type of coaching thinking we hope to foster. Effective coaches need to automatically link how someone acts with the goal the company wants to achieve.

Getting Things Done in a Complex Environment

We're continually seeing people who did fine when they could rely on their role and hierarchy to accomplish tasks but stumble when they have to rely on their influence, vision, and ability to mobilize a group. The complexity of working globally and at a time when people (especially the new generation of recruits) question authority often requires managers to get things done indirectly; they need to facilitate solutions through people who aren't always direct reports.

As a result of this complexity, people often respond with one or more of the fourteen behaviors discussed previously. Or rather, the complexity drives them to rely on a particular behavior that is inappropriate and ineffective. For instance, a manager faced with a bewildering team sponsorship assignment attempts to bully the team toward a solution. Or an executive struggling to weave his way through the esoteric customs and culture of a Third World country shows the inflexibility of a perfectionist.

Organizations desperately need their members to work effectively in these complex environments. You can lead them to understand how the complexity of their environments is linked to their problematic behaviors, facilitating their awareness of why they're doing what they're doing. By providing them with an opportunity to reflect, to test assumptions, to consider other options, and to reframe their perspective, you give people tools and insights to deal with this complexity.

Common and unproductive behaviors to watch for:

False advocates react by feigning comfort with and acceptance of working through influence and indirection while trying to get things done the old-fashioned way.

Hyper-moody types alternate bursts of temper with an almost comatose acceptance when asked to confront difficult, confusing issues.

Small-picture thinkers work harder and longer than ever at technical tasks in order to escape the complexity that big-picture thinking demands.

Reconciling Paradoxical Situations and Issues

Many unproductive behaviors stem from the maddening paradoxes that lurk in every nook and cranny of work life: meeting long-term and short-term goals, satisfying local and global imperatives, delivering results while maintaining values, developing your own talent and "buying" it from the outside. It's maddening to live in the paradox rather than choose black or white. The reflex action of many managers is to figure out the specs and act in a goal-focused way. Paradox makes this impossible. Management has seen people who are uncomfortable with paradox leave or make major mistakes, and they know the value of paradox-friendly managers. Sometimes managers look upward and "demand" clear strategies, directions, or measures from the top management, forgetting that they are paid to figure a situation out and deliver results closer to the action.

Common and unproductive behaviors to watch for:

Team wreckers surround themselves with people who provide them with unflinching support and loyalty; they attempt to ignore the paradox.

The transition-challenged become especially flustered and even dysfunctional when they're thrust into new positions or companies where the paradox level is high; they're so uncomfortable that they make decisions too fast or too slowly, become depressed, or take out their frustration on direct reports.

Cynics snipe at, complain about, and criticize their paradoxes; they prefer to give paradox a verbal slap than to come to terms with their environment's realities.

Empathizing and Responding in Ways That Meet People's Needs

Given today's diverse workforce, companies must have managers who possess emotional intelligence. It's no longer possible for managers to manage everyone one way. The most effective executives are those who can use their intuition and communication skills to grasp what motivates others and adapt their style accordingly. In a fascinating recent study, American and Japanese managers were asked to draw what came to mind when they heard the word *organization*. Most of the Americans drew buildings or products; the Japanese drew people. The Americans' visual symbols are indicative of a society that is very good at reading things and not so good at reading people.

Common and unproductive behaviors to watch for:

Egotists act as if they know exactly what each person in their group needs — they look at others' needs through their own; they falsely believe they understand what motivates each and every one of their direct reports, relying on their egos rather than their empathy or communication skills.

Bullies overreact and try and tell everyone what they need and what should motivate them.

Upstagers give the impression that they're intuitive and empathetic but in fact lack these skills; they try and fake it and may succeed until they're put in a position where they really do have to empathize with people to achieve objectives.

Making Innovation and Creativity Happen

In a knowledge-based world, companies depend on growing their intellectual assets. Management, therefore, is anxious for its current and future leaders to bring out their people's best ideas. We've found that this is a formidable task for many managers. They are bewildered by the process, unable to determine when brainstorming is called for or when the making of ideas should be less free-form. We've coached partners of a major accounting firm in this area, and they have had tremendous difficulty fostering creativity. Many are unable to share knowledge and solicit ideas from their clients, feeling as if they're giving up control in exchange for synergetic thinking; it doesn't strike them as a fair exchange for creativity and goes against their training and instincts.

Common and unproductive behaviors to watch for:

Worriers often offer excuses for avoiding innovation and creativity because they are afraid of change.

Perfectionists spend most of their time and energy polishing the details to a fine sheen; they're creative in the tiny ways in which they emphasize and enforce the rules and regulations, thinking they've fulfilled management's mandate.

Pleasers are creative and innovative in safe ways; they might talk a good game and document how much time they've spent brainstorming and doing creativity exercises, but they're unwilling to take the risks that true creativity demands.

Adapting to New Roles or Levels

CEOs and other top executives frequently complain about resistant, stubborn, or inflexible managers. Whether consciously or not, these managers dig in their heels and fail to adapt to new realities. We've coached a number of managers at a major clothing manufacturer who are implementing a new strategy of selling direct to consumers (as opposed to only selling to traditional retailers). They can no longer manage inventory as in the past or respond in a leisurely way to orders. They must now understand Internet and other technologies. However, some of these managers have made only token efforts at adapting, hoping that direct-to-consumer selling will not be important.

We've also coached people who have moved from functional to general manager roles, and they've struggled mightily. For instance, one marketing executive simply couldn't leave his marketing mindset behind. He preferred hanging out with marketing people; he found it difficult to talk the language of operational people. When quality control problems developed, he tried to solve them through marketing tactics. It was an illogical but inevitable response. He simply was falling back on his strength in a time of crisis rather than being flexible and trying to learn a new approach.

Common and unproductive behaviors to watch for:

The transition-challenged are especially vulnerable here, becoming closed-off, distrustful, and angry when thrust into roles that require them to shift their workstyles.

The team wrecker brings inappropriate people with him when he moves to a new position or finds a way to alienate the people who are already in place when he takes on the new assignment.

The upstager surprises everyone with her inability to make the shift; she successfully handled less visible new roles in the past, but she is out of her depth when she's called on to adapt her style and attitude in significant ways.

Reading the Environment

Companies can no longer afford leaders who don't pick up on signals—political, marketplace, technological, and other messages being sent by their environments. They bring Action Coaches in to help people develop this "reading" skill. This type of coaching involves teaching people to pay attention, to keep eyes and ears open so that emerging trends and developing coalitions don't escape their notice, and to develop their own point of view about the data. Sometimes this means helping people sift through information to discern whether a technological breakthrough will have an impact on their industry. Sometimes it means helping them manage the responses of various camps when they need to build a coalition to achieve a new organizational goal.

Companies now need people who are sensitive to unfolding political realities and trends. We coached a top executive named Aaron who headed a large manufacturing division that was doing very well domestically. His boss, however, wanted Aaron to help the division build a global franchise and gave him this as a goal. To achieve this goal, Aaron needed the cooperation and support of the company's regional operating heads throughout the world. These operation heads also reported to Aaron's boss, but this boss continued to drive them on revenue targets and operating profit. Thus, Aaron couldn't enlist them in the effort to achieve a communal goal; he needed to read the politics of the situation and find a way to involve these operating heads in helping him achieve his global goal.

Common and unproductive behaviors to watch for:

The transition-challenged misses signs and signals that might be obvious to him in other situations; he has such trouble changing jobs or moving to a new level that he fails to read the political climate and offends a key player—a player who is key to his success in the new position.

The cynic becomes flustered by volatile internal issues as well as changing external environments; he micromanages his environment rather than trying to read it; he tries to control things (which is impossible) rather than to anticipate and be proactive.

The worrier may be able to read the environment but what he reads is so disturbing to his sensibility that he finds excuses to dismiss what he sees.

Managing Change

We include this final management imperative, recognizing that it's a broad category that overlaps some of the others we've mentioned. Still, it remains of paramount concern to leaders of most corporations. Despite all the courses, books, articles, and other tools out there, many bright, effective managers still have trouble creating the need for change, creating the conditions for change, or dealing with resistance to change.

Common and unproductive behaviors to watch for:

The small-picture thinker becomes increasingly technical in his focus, retreating to the details he knows in order to avoid the change-related problems he doesn't.

The upstager gives the appearance of change management competency, but the illusion is shattered when she fails to deal effectively with a major, spotlighted change initiative.

This is the perfect scenario for the false advocate to feign acceptance and support of a change program and then find a way to ignore or even sabotage that program.

See Exhibit 4.2 for a summary of how coaching must take place on two levels: the individual level and the organizational level.

Keeping Behaviors and Business Requirements in Mind

After coaching this way over a period of time, this two-level thinking will become second nature. Until then, use the following checklist to keep yourself on a dual track:

Take "breaks" during the coaching process that allow you and your client to reflect on the issues involved; don't problem solve yourself to death and lose sight of larger business issues.

Keep your own coaching journal that documents what you talked about with the person you're coaching; have a column for business requirements discussed and one for behaviors and development issues. Is there an imbalance between the two?

Refer to our Coaching Tips about which behaviors and categories are often a volatile mix.

Avoid jumping to simplistic conclusions or solutions; a simplistic approach often involves only behaviors or business requirements.

Think holistically about any coaching situation; consider all the other factors that may affect individual behaviors and organizational requirements, including the problematic

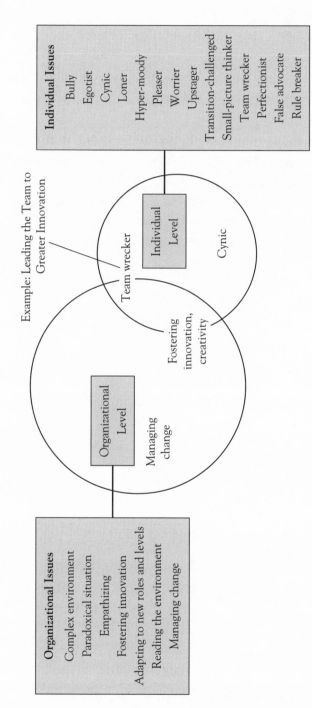

Organizational Issues

Complex environment
Paradoxical situation
Empathizing
Fostering innovation
Adapting to new roles and levels
Reading the environment
Managing change

Organizational Level

Managing change

Fostering innovation, creativity

Team wrecker

Example: Leading the Team to Greater Innovation

Individual Level

Cynic

Individual Issues

Bully
Egotist
Cynic
Loner
Hyper-moody
Pleaser
Worrier
Upstager
Transition-challenged
Small-picture thinker
Team wrecker
Perfectionist
False advocate
Rule breaker

Exhibit 4.2. Action Coaching: Thinking on Two Levels.

behaviors of others (boss, customers, direct reports), the competitive environment (resulting in tremendous pressure for performance), or the career aspirations of the individual and personal crises (for example, a divorce).

What you'll discover from thinking on two levels is that there's a gap between an individual's behaviors and an organization's requirements. To close that gap may require a bit of self-awareness or a major transformation. How to close that gap—to move someone to a desired action—is the subject of the next chapter.

5

Motivating Change

If people weren't so complicated, it would be easy to get them to cease and desist from the behaviors discussed in the previous chapter and respond to organizational imperatives. They would stop relying on tried-and-true approaches and foster creativity because the organization would offer them more money, power, or other incentives to do so. Or they would bring in coaches who could help traditionalists see the error of their ways, and this new self-awareness would produce the changes the organization seeks.

As you may know, these simplistic approaches to human behavior are all too common. Your organization has probably attempted to motivate people to raise their productivity or meet a deadline by offering bonuses, trips, or other carrots — or by raising the specter of the stick (firings or negative performance reviews). You may also have tried to "fix" people through executive development programs or management training. At best these are temporary fixes; they might get people to do what the organization wants but without any real belief or energy. It creates a transactional relationship between individuals and their organizations and assumes that people are all the same and motivated by the same things.

There are better ways to make the linkage between behavior and organizational goals and motivate people to change in ways that are permanent and productive. This is the essence of Action Coaching.

The Secret Behind Motivation

If you were to eavesdrop on some executives frustrated by the poor performance of a team or the inability of an individual to adjust to a new environment, you might conclude that the underperforming people were not a good fit, unambitious, lacking in talent, or stubborn. Some executives jump to conclusions in the heat of the moment about why people don't do what they're "supposed" to do.

In fact, people do what they do for very good reasons. We've rarely encountered anyone who was purposely trying to do a poor or even an average job. Most people believe they are doing their jobs the right way and that they'll achieve their goals if they just persist in their behaviors. You need to get into the heads of these people. As you gather information and conduct interviews, you need to get a sense of why they're acting like a fussbudget or a yes-person; you need to understand the rationale for their behaviors.

What drives people? What makes them excel in some areas and not in others? Why does this person always seem to fall short of his potential? Why did he do so well in his last job and not in this one?

It boils down to figuring out what might motivate an individual to change and linking that motivation to organizational goals. Contrary to what many people might believe, it's difficult if not impossible to change a person's motivation. If someone is intrinsically motivated by power, you can't appeal to his sense of loyalty to the company or sense of solidarity with his team. What you can do is discover that he's motivated by power and link that to a larger goal. For instance, help him see that if he can achieve his group's mission, he'll satisfy that sense of power because he'll have the opportunity to expand his group into new areas.

These insights are difficult for individuals to come by on their own. People may have trouble understanding how the latest change initiative will meet their professional growth needs or satisfy their desire for a more challenging assignment. Or rather, they don't understand the specific connections between what's driving them and what's driving the business. If you can make that connection come alive for a client, you can help him achieve significant performance breakthroughs and transformations.

In their rush to get key people up to speed, organizations often ignore the issue of motivation altogether, assuming that it's obvious how responding to an organizational imperative will benefit the individual — usually relying on the compensation system to motivate everyone. Even worse, companies often naively assume that the reason someone isn't performing up to snuff or is making mistakes is due solely to a lack of skill. In other words, managers will change their behaviors and do a better job of managing a diverse workforce if they take diversity training. Although it's true they may need to acquire some skills, that's usually only one part of the story.

A number of years ago, the CEO of Honeywell decided that he wanted his top executives — all of whom were engineers like the CEO — to learn about and implement the science of human behavior. The CEO was convinced that if his technically talented people could learn to establish better relationships using psychological tools, they would be far more effective in their jobs. The CEO made it clear to his people how important learning this new skill was; he hired coaches to help them acquire it and gave them the time and resources to do so. Despite all this, most of them remained engineers and scientists who were still suspicious of the psychological sciences and were unable or unwilling to put human behavioral tools and lessons to use.

The problem was motivation. Even in this command-and-control era, the CEO's insistence that this was important was insufficient motivation. Today, some companies usually know better and attempt to motivate new behaviors in various ways. The problem is that they try and create *new* motivations. They pay no attention to individual needs and drivers when crafting the carrot or stick that is designed to change behaviors.

Don't create new motivation. Instead, as a coach figure out how to arrange the environment to satisfy an individual's existing motivation. Produce a set of conditions or relationships that lead to behavioral change by identifying what the motivation is. Provide feedback, share information, and use "what if" scenarios and other tools to help clients discover a good reason to change attitudes and behaviors. Let's examine the three basic patterns of motivation and how you can determine which one is driving someone you're coaching.

Three Patterns of Motivation

Professor David McClelland of Harvard University did a great deal of formative research on motivation during the 1970s, and he came up with the following three patterns: (1) achievement, (2) power-control, and (3) affiliation.[1] Each pattern has many variations and can change over time and the course of a career. Still, understanding the general traits of each pattern and how they manifest themselves will help you identify them.

Achievement

These individuals are driven by a desire to do well in their jobs and their careers. They are not moved by empty praise or undeserved promotions but want to reach challenging goals. They want to be recognized for a job well done, and they're acutely aware when their performance falls below their own high standards. As managers, these achievers often fail to motivate others; they assume that their direct reports are internally motivated, just as they are. They often are parsimonious with praise, believing their people should know when they've done a good job.

---

[1] McClelland, D., *The Achieving Society* (New York: Van Nostrand Reinhold, 1954).

Power-Control

Here the pattern involves a desire to shape others and have an impact on other people and the environment. These people often build significant influence bases within organizations, but they also create a certain amount of distrust, envy, and fear among those who work for them. Managers who are in this motivational pattern may be manipulative, and they may also find it difficult to function effectively on teams or in other situations where their control is decreased.

Affiliation

In this pattern, people are motivated by the need to be liked and achieve satisfaction by being in relationships with other people. Affiliaters place tremendous emphasis on how others perceive them and the recognition they receive. As managers, they're often well liked by the people who work for them, but they probably aren't respected (or feared) and don't use power effectively.

Deceptive Patterns

No matter how perceptive you are as a coach, it's not always easy to spot the motivation pattern that's dominant in a given individual, especially because it is influenced by life or career stage. If you ask Sharon what drives her—affiliation, power, or achievement—she might respond that achievement is what she's after. In reality, Sharon might be embarrassed to tell you that what she really craves is power and impact. Or she might not know what is pushing her. Complicating matters is that most people have a mixture of affiliation, power, and achievement motivators and that one of these is more compelling than the other two.

Many coaches overlook unearthing key motivators; they assume that human resources or their client's boss must come up with a good motivational tool or tactic. But as a coach your job is to discover existing motivation and use it to link up with organizational imperatives. If Sharon is driven by power and the company wants her to be more comfortable managing in a paradoxical environment, you need to find a way to show her that she'll obtain more power if she responds to this organizational need.

Before we get to how to do so, let's talk about how you can identify the dominant motivational pattern. As you begin gathering data from your client and others, the following five-step process might prove helpful.

First, look for clues in your client's personal—not just professional—life. Sometimes, revealing information can be gleaned by asking a client to talk about his or her hobbies, educational background, family, and so on. You might find, for instance, that a woman is a member of numerous clubs and other organizations (affiliation), or that another client is the president of his local alumni association (affiliation), or another is captain of a sports team (power-control). Or you might discover that the individual was a straight-A student in school or has a goal of climbing the tallest mountain on each of seven continents (achievement).

Second, ask people to tell you what their single most disappointing or humbling experience has been in their career. Sometimes it's easier to see what motivates people when you look at what they didn't achieve than at what they did. For instance, if someone says her biggest disappointment was not being selected for an important team, that might suggest affiliation as the main motivator.

Third, give clients a word test. The following test is designed to get past people's conscious (and possibly misleading) thoughts about what motivates them and move to a deeper, more honest level. The following groups of words relate to each of the motivational patterns. Jumble them up and have people circle the ones that "feel right." Emphasize that this is an intuitive exercise and they should react rather than think when making their responses. Achievement words are *goals, hard work, valedictorian, higher level, accomplishment, objectives, challenge, extra credit, gold medal, fast track, bonus, pay-for-play.* Power-control words are *influence, authority, impact, quarterback, force, mentor, boss, energy, shape, leader, decision maker.* Affiliation words are *team, respect, cohesion, consensus, likable, group, mutual, alliance, partner, synergy.*

Fourth, find out why clients want what they say they want. In other words, learn what's underneath their statement of what they hope to achieve in an organization or in their career. Why do they want to become head of the information technology department? Why do they want to be the company's top salesperson? Why do they want to work for IBM? If you listen to their explanations, you may hear what's really driving them. For instance, "I want to be the company's top salesperson because it will mean I've reached the ultimate goal for salespeople in this company" could indicate the achievement motivator.

Fifth and last, ask clients to describe a peak experience—a time in their life or career in which they felt "on the edge," using their talents in a memorable and satisfying way. Dissect this edge experience carefully to uncover the underlying elements of passion, strong interest, and therefore motive.

Communicating the Gap

Once you know someone's motivation pattern, you must find the leverage to move them from point A to point B. You can help them see the same old issues in a brilliant new light so that they're motivated to change their behaviors. Show or tell them how they can satisfy their inner drive while also achieving what the organization wants. For instance, Sam is a marketing executive with a pharmaceutical company, and he's been having trouble managing in an increasingly complex environment. The direct-to-consumer advertising trend has thrown him for a loop, and he's finding that the marketing message he wants to communicate is being weighted down with a load of legally mandated qualifiers. As a result, his loner behavior has intensified, and he's been working behind closed doors too much and with his team too little.

What helped Sam change his loner behavior was coaching that zeroed in on what motivated him. He wanted control; he needed to bring some order and logic to his work life and feel as if he could exert some influence on how products—especially new products—sold. We helped Sam see how he could only regain this control if he began to work with a variety of people. We showed how he needed to get out of his office and form alliances with consultants who understood direct-to-consumer advertising, ad agencies, and others. We introduced him to another executive at another pharmaceutical company who had struggled with a similar transition, and this executive told Sam how the various alliances he had forged enabled him to have greater impact on product marketing, although it was a different sort of impact than he had had in the past.

For Sam, there was a gap between his loner behavior and the organizationally desired ability to manage in complex environments. Once we made him aware of this gap, Sam started to change his behaviors. You need to hold up the gap for your clients to see.

This gap isn't as simple as it sounds. It can involve the following variations. The gap may be (1) between who an individual is and who the organization wants him to be, (2) between who an individual is and who he wants to be, or (3) between who an individual is and who he might be ideally.

In addition, sometimes the gap is a result of organizational prejudices or beliefs—what we refer to as a preference gap. Organizations sometimes implicitly ask this question: Why can't a woman be more like a man? They don't ask it directly, of course. But some male leaders unconsciously fear that women who are promoted into management positions may fail to exert control, make decisions, or take command. They fear they're too focused on involving people and reaching consensus. When men dominate management ranks, these preference gaps can emerge, which reflect the preferred style of those in charge and make achieving diversity an "unconscious challenge."

Paradox gaps sometimes arise from seemingly contradictory requirements. For instance, Hal believes in achieving a balance between work and family, but his organization is demanding more of his time than ever before and asking him to do a great deal of traveling, which reveals the importance of balance to Hal. The gap may be the result of a paradox rather than a contradiction. Hal may have overestimated the amount of time that is required for him to do what the organization wishes.

Skill gaps are quite common and relatively easy to address. The difference between who people are and who their organization wants them to be relates to a missing skill. Action Coaching focuses on helping people develop needed skills through rehearsal, practice, insight, direct feedback, and other methods.

Perception gaps involve people who aren't performing in ways the organization desires because they don't perceive the possibility of that type of performance. For instance, a manager persists in pushing decisions upward, even though management has empowered him to make decisions and needs him to do so quickly and effectively. For years this manager has witnessed how his hierarchical company functions; he doesn't believe that they've changed or that he really has the authority necessary to make major decisions without getting three superiors to sign off on them.

To close this gap, demonstrate the "new realities" for your clients. Benchmark how other organizations have shifted from hierarchical structures to flattened ones or provide other evidence that this shift is possible. We worked with the president of a global telecommunications company and helped him form a team of "smart dummies," that is, people who knew little about the project to which they were being assigned. The idea was that they would bring a fresh perspective to the project. When we were talking about who to put on this team, the president balked when we argued that a particularly powerful executive should not be included on it. The president knew that if he didn't include this executive, he'd receive a great deal of flak. In the past, he'd always included her on teams such as this one, not only because she contributed great ideas but because she'd raise a ruckus if she were left out. The perception gap for him was that he could never leave this executive off an important team. By breaking his existing frame, we demonstrated that the world would not end and he would survive if he left her off the team.

Existential gaps develop when someone's behavior is limited by fear or by concerns about having a place in the world of work. "Is this all there is?" a high-achieving manager might ask at the prime of his career. Another manager might become apathetic because she feels that the fun and challenge have gone out of her work life. As a result of this existential apathy or even despair, people don't respond to organizational imperatives. The gap between who they are and who they might be is a result of intangible and philosophical issues. Find a way to help these existentialists reinvent their work life. Direct them toward new challenges: have them take on fresh projects, change their job description, or even move to a new position or job level.

Breaking Frame: A Good Way to Close the Gap

As difficult as it sometimes is, you must push and prod your clients to look at things differently. You'll find that people routinely deny the gaps that exist at work or they resist doing anything about them. Sometimes it takes more than understanding words and restating the situation for people to change.

Sometimes you need to assume the role of provocateur. You must jar people out of their old way of viewing the world and offer alternative visions. Reframing is an important tool in this regard, and you can use it along with reflection, visioning, and feedback to motivate clients. Or rather, you can use it to help clients understand how their needs and the organization's align, thus recharging their motivational batteries. Set your sites high if that's what's necessary. If someone needs to be motivated to transform himself, then that should govern your coaching. Sometimes reframing involves serious confrontations and deeply emotional experiences. It's not easy to catalyze someone to reframe his vision of himself and his organization, and that's why you shouldn't hesitate to push people hard if that's what's required.

Here are two approaches you might employ to help people you're coaching reframe their thinking:

• *Use the why-not line of questions.* When you find that people are offering all sorts of excuses about why they can't do something or change a particular behavior, respond with a series of why-nots. An executive told us that he didn't have any time and that he lacked the flexibility to operate differently because he was responsible for overseeing two hundred monthly reports. We asked him if could reduce the number of reports, and he said he couldn't. Why not?, we asked. He explained how each report served a valuable purpose. Why not eliminate certain reports?, we suggested? Why not do what Company X did when they cut their monthly reports in half? Why not test doing away with certain reports or condensing some of them for a month and see what happens? As you can tell, these why-nots are not just verbal, they're demonstrated in various ways. Action Coaching requires persistent questioning about what could be done, and it helps to be armed with the latest data from "global best practice" companies.

• *Push the limits.* Sometimes you need to surprise or even shock clients by showing them how the boundaries they've set up in their minds are illusory. When they talk about the high costs of inventory, tell them about a company that has done away with inventory altogether. When they talk about their fears of taking risks, introduce them to an inveterate risk taker who has succeeded, despite his gambler's mentality. By pushing the limits, you may well extend the gap initially. The organization may want a manager to foster level-three creativity, but you demonstrate all the benefits and attainability of level-one creativity. The gap widens, but so too might the incentive to close it. Sometimes you have to set people's sights higher for them to become energized about changing who they are and how they work.

Motivational Mistakes: Closing the Wrong Gap

A certain amount of "precision" is necessary in your motivational efforts. You can't be satisfied with just coaching a client to change a behavior or develop a new skill or attitude. Yes, you've created action through your coaching, but it may not be exactly the right action. As a result, you may fall short of the mark. Your client may feel he's made progress, but this progress doesn't improve business results or prepare him for an important new role in the company.

Be alert for common coaching mistakes in this area — times when you've helped people change so that it just *seems* like the gap has closed between who they are and what the organization needs them to be. In reality, you've closed another gap that has little organizational or business results impact. The following are the most frequent errors coaches make in this regard:

• *Closing the gap between who someone is and where he wants to be in his career.* The organizational requirements are ignored, and a person changes in ways that may well help him develop more marketable career skills but not the skills that allow him to lead his team more effectively.

To avoid this mistake, make sure you distinguish the skill someone yearns to develop from the ones that a larger corporate group needs him to develop. If necessary, make a chart of career-enhancing skills versus organization-enhancing ones. If a skill lands on both lists, that makes your motivational job that much easier. As a coach, you must balance the interests of the company and the individual. As an Action Coach, you must find the way to make them converge.

• *Closing the gap between who someone is and who your personal bias dictates a client should become.* In other words, both you and your client misperceive what will really contribute to the client's value to the team or department. Perhaps you're coaching a direct report whom you're grooming for a leadership position, and you're convinced he needs to become assertive because of your observations of him in action. In fact, he's plenty assertive around everyone but you, and his real leadership development challenges lie elsewhere.

To avoid this mistake, talk to others (people you manage, a boss, someone who has coached you) about how your own attitudes and needs may be affecting the goals you set for a client.

• *Closing the gap between who someone is and an illusory business requirement.* Coaches become convinced that people need to become faster or more innovative, team-oriented, or global in their thinking. These are all trendy traits, but they may not be ones that serve your organization as well as others; you end up developing someone for an ideal rather than a real company.

To avoid this mistake, make sure you get plenty of feedback and direction, especially from your bosses or others in management. Don't make facile assumptions about leadership traits or the qualities that make team players. Test your assumptions through conversations with others. For example, although managers today are exhorted to be fast and make speedy decisions, it may be better to wait until the last possible moment before making a decision in order to get the best information available.

• *Closing the gap between who someone is and the new behavior everyone wishes he would develop.* People sometimes exhibit behaviors that are irritating, obnoxious, and just plain weird. Naturally, you wish they would learn to correct this behavior and become more "normal." That's fine, but changing this behavior may have no impact on business results; it may simply make someone less obnoxious. Although there are times when being less obnoxious can have an impact on a team or business, there are also times when the desire to change someone is purely personal.

To avoid this mistake, project how someone might better meet a business requirement by changing a behavior. Be specific to the point of listing all ways a changed behavior might contribute to a performance objective or help someone fulfill a crucial new role. In our experience, sometimes the true change agents in a company receive negative 360-degree feedback—for a good reason. They are taking their team or company somewhere it resists going.

How to Assess Your Chances of Success

Remember, you're not just trying to help someone change; you're trying to help them change in very specific, business-oriented ways. Although we believe all people are capable of making these behavioral changes, not all of them are ready or willing to do so.

Evaluate the specific individual and situation. Each assignment comes with different degrees of difficulty. If, for instance, you're trying to transform an introvert into an extrovert, you have your work cut out for you. If you're attempting to help a manager become comfortable managing globally and he's never been outside the United States and is burdened with prejudices about Europeans and Asians, then it's going to be a battle to achieve this performance breakthrough.

Pinpoint the goal level as early in the process as possible. If you know that you're after a highly ambitious performance breakthrough for your client, you and your client need to understand that the process is going to take a significant amount of time and effort. You need to make sure you have the cooperation of management to help you achieve your coaching goals. They must be willing to give you the time and resources (access to other people, provision of a positive career path if your client develops in the direction the company wants, and so on) that will support your coaching. If, however, all that's required is self-awareness, your motivational job is more easily managed and you don't have to use all sorts of tools and spend a lot of coaching time to achieve the desired business results.

A variety of factors affect your chances of coaching success. Some people will respond positively to your motivational efforts and others will resist like crazy, regardless of what level of change you want them to make. Ascertain this acceptance or resistance in Step 1 (determining what needs to happen) or 2 (establishing trust and mutual expectations) of the coaching process and tailor your motivational efforts accordingly. If the resistance is strong, recognize that the person may not be worth the coaching effort. The questions in Exhibit 5.1 are designed to help you evaluate the chances that your coaching will work. The more yes responses you mark down, the more likely clients are to respond positively.

Exhibit 5.1. Determining How Successful Action Coaching Will Be.

	Yes	No
1. Are candidates in a new set of circumstances—new job, new region, new relationships—that make them eager for help?	❏	❏
2. Are they sending signals of distress—telling their boss or HR that they want to attend seminars, take training, be transferred, and so forth?	❏	❏
3. Are there leverage points in the situation? Is a given individual being considered for a promotion, membership on a highly visible team, or such?	❏	❏
4. Are the candidates open to learning, new ideas, new information?	❏	❏
5. Do they have a track record of being able to adapt and change?	❏	❏
6. Do candidates have other people in the organization—bosses, teams—who will support your efforts?	❏	❏
7. Is there a clear, presenting problem, a sense of urgency, and a pressing need for change?	❏	❏
8. Has the organization or the candidate's boss provided clear direction or goals for successful change; have they established explicit measures for the candidate?	❏	❏
9. Is it reasonable to expect that someone could acquire a missing skill in the time frame set by the organization?	❏	❏
10. Are candidates being asked to make changes in behavior that seem feasible, given their behavior in the past, or are they being asked to make a Jekyll-and-Hyde transformation?	❏	❏

Part III

Coaching One-to-One

6

The First Meeting

Coaching is often messy. You should be prepared for a first meeting in which the issues aren't particularly clear, the goals you're faced with seem contradictory (between what an individual wants and an organization wants for him), and the way to begin escapes you.

To help you start out on the right foot, let's examine some of the initial issues you need to confront as a coach. What you know for sure at the beginning of this process is that you've decided (or someone has decided for you) that a given individual needs to be coached. If you're a manager who wants to coach a direct report, you may have made this decision because you're convinced this high-potential individual can contribute even more to your group's performance by growing in a new area. Or it's possible that you've been assigned to coach someone by a boss who is concerned about this individual's counterproductive behaviors. In either case, you're driven by a behavior problem or a development opportunity that seems simple enough on the surface but often becomes muddled once you delve into it.

To understand the complexities you'll face, pretend you've just been given a coaching assignment. You're called into your boss's office because he's concerned about Mary and wants you to coach her. As he explains:

For the past year, Mary has really been stymied in her attempts to finish assignments on time and effectively. She's been with us for eight years, but since the new CEO took over and really transformed the company's policies and culture, Mary's been lost. She just doesn't understand the new political realities. She steps on the wrong people's toes, she doesn't really get how to put a sponsored team together, she seems completely ignorant of the CEO's key issues. One time, Mary was in a meeting attended by the CEO and she started talking about reengineering. Well, the CEO hates that term, hates all the connotations of the concept. But Mary's oblivious, and I swear I could see the steam rising from the CEO's neck. Mary's very talented and has done good work in the past, but she needs to develop political savvy—fast.

So you start out knowing that the boss wants Mary to develop political savvy. But there are a million other things you don't know. First and foremost, how does the development of political savvy fit into larger organizational imperatives or goals? If Mary becomes savvy, will she be in a better position to help her group reach key new objectives that fit into the company's business strategy? Or will it just make her less embarrassing to bring to meetings—which would just reinforce the current culture. Most important of all, how does Mary feel about these questions?

To make sense of this situation, you need to have a broader perspective on what's taking place, both inside Mary's head and in her environment. To gain this perspective, you need to meet with her and ask questions, listen, empathize, and learn.

Deconstructing Mary

To achieve some clarification about what's going on with Mary and what actions will benefit both her and the organization, you can ask the following questions:

• *Where is the assessment that Mary is not politically savvy coming from?* Is it only Mary's boss who sees her this way? Do other people think she's very savvy? Does Mary herself believe she has political smarts? Is the manifestation of her political naiveté that she's getting into trouble with key organizational power figures? Does she fail to show up at the right events? Does she refuse to "lower" herself and play games such as networking and currying favor with the right people? Many people in organizations take great pride in speaking their mind no matter who their words might offend or in never doing anything (taking the right people to lunch, attending a social function) unless it directly relates to their work. Is Mary's lack of political savvy willful, stemming from her ideology rather than her idiocy?

Interpreting the answers. One of the tricks of achieving clarity involves separating appearances from reality. As a coach, you cannot afford to take one person's word for granted, even if it's the word of a top executive. If everyone agrees that Mary is a political babe in the woods and she could improve her performance with some political training or mentoring, then your course is clear. If, however, you hear different opinions about Mary's political smarts, then don't be so quick to assume that what you heard at first is correct. See if you can detect a pattern in the responses to these source questions. Perhaps all the new employees feel she lacks political smarts, whereas the old ones disagree. Listen for opinions that cluster together based on management rank, department, and other divisions.

• *What are the effects of Mary's behavior?* In other words, what are the negative repercussions for both Mary and the people she works with? When people understand how what they say and do hurts their careers or causes problems for their group, they're much more motivated to change. We worked with one executive who wasn't willing to change until he realized that his lack of political savvy was preventing his team from receiving visibility and exposure for their accomplishments. When we made this problem crystal clear, the executive began to change his behavior. If Mary is

reasonably receptive, you might try out some of the feedback you've
heard on her and see how she responds.

Interpreting the responses. Focus on feedback that suggests tangible, measurable effects. In other words, look for very specific,
negative repercussions of Mary's actions. You'll probably hear many
general complaints and comments, and these won't be of much use
to you or Mary. What will be motivating for Mary are concrete instances of negative behaviors that you can play back for her.

• *What are the reasons for Mary's lack of savvy?* Coaches can
easily jump to conclusions about why people are acting the way
they are. For instance, the coach might think at first that Mary isn't
good with politics because she spent years working in an apolitical
climate and never developed this skill. In fact, Mary might not be
good at politics for any one of ten or twenty reasons. She might be
a natural loner, preferring to work in isolation. She might be surprised to hear herself called politically naive; she simply hasn't been
aware of the importance of working the system. The issue might involve Mary's candor and openness—when she speaks her mind,
she fails to realize that she's alienating important people. Identifying the reason for someone's behavioral problems may take some
time, but it's great if you can glimpse it at the beginning.

Interpreting the responses. You'll find it helpful to list the reasons
and determine which ones are actionable. If she's really not politically savvy, it's probably for a number of reasons, and some of them
may be impossible or very difficult to understand or change. If Mary
is just a generally naive person, then your coaching goal is nothing
less than transformation. If she simply hasn't adapted to the new
culture, that may be easier to remedy.

• *What is the organization's objective in helping Mary deal with her
lack of savvy?* Sometimes the reason is not as obvious as it might appear, and Mary herself may not understand the point. She may believe the company just wants her to be like everyone else; she may
think they're all a bunch of sharks and they want her to become one
too. Or she may think that management is biased against women
executives and wants to turn them into game-playing men. If Mary

understands the real organizational objective—to make her savvy enough so she can take on more responsibility and be involved in an important new business strategy—then she may become more enthusiastic about the process. Or she may not, which raises a new coaching challenge: What does Mary want?

Interpreting the responses. The key here is to reduce the objective to terms that make sense to Mary. If the objective is simply to be "less politically naive," then Mary may find that to be a silly objective. But if you discover that the underlying need is for Mary to become more astute about manipulating the system to get the resources her team needs, that could be a more compelling objective. (See Exhibit 6.1 for questions you might ask; the answers will help you understand a client's situation.)

Answers to these four questions will help you determine whether the problem resides on the surface or whether it's buried deeper. You might find that everything is very clear about what needs to be done to help a person change to meet an organizational imperative during this first meeting; you can identify specific actions that should be taken. In other instances, you may discover that the problems

---

Exhibit 6.1. Assessment Questions.

1. Where is the assessment of the person coming from? (the boss, the person, other sources?)
   - What behaviors led to these perceptions?
   - What is the intention behind the person's behaviors?
2. What are the effects of the person's behavior?
   - What are the negative repercussions for the person and others?
3. What are the reasons for the person's behavior?
4. Is the person aware of the behavior?
5. Is the behavior intentional?
6. Is it a "why" issue—a matter of principle?
7. Is it a "what" issue—a habit or workstyle preference?
8. What is the organization's objective in helping the person change?

are more complex—that an inability to manage globally or a re-luctance to work across boundaries is rooted in personal issues.

The point is that what you discover will determine the speed and manner in which you can implement the rest of the Action Coaching process. During this initial interaction, you should also think about whether a client's issue relates to "what" or "why." In many instances, coaching is easier and faster when the issue is *what* someone does rather than *why* she does it. For instance, if Mary has a "what" issue, she may simply need expert guidance in what the politics of the company are and how to play them. If Mary has a "why" issue, she may feel it's beneath her to play politics. In that case, she will require much more feedback, advice, and interven-tion by coaches to shift her behaviors.

Overcoming Resistance

When resistance is high, the coaching process slows down. If you're lucky and discover your client is highly receptive to learning, you will have made a valuable discovery. You can move forward with relative speed and ease. If you know that management supports coaching and, in fact, has positioned coaching as a way to facilitate development, you're likely to find more receptivity. Resistance is more common when coaching is perceived to be an intervention designed to deal with problematic behaviors.

To help you determine the ease and the speed at which you can implement coaching right from the start, let's examine two relevant issues: (1) the typical range of reactions of coaching candidates and (2) the factors that determine someone's readiness to be coached.

Range of Reactions

Concern or Fear

In some people's minds, coaching is a signal that something has gone wrong with their jobs. If their company has a history of using coach-ing only to deal with people's negative behaviors rather than as a development tool, they're especially skittish about being brought into a coaching situation. Although some people respond positively to this concern and are eager to be coached, others react with fear and resist the process; they view being coached as a black mark on their record.

Denial

These coaching candidates react by denying that anything is wrong or that they need any type of help, even if the help is developmental and geared toward selection or a leadership opportunity. Some of these people are offended by coaching, insisting that there isn't anything they can't do. Others refuse to admit that their performance has declined. Still others translate their denial into blaming other people and situations for their problems. These people set up formidable defenses, and it's tough for coaches to get through to them.

Skepticism

This reaction is certainly less intense than denial, but it's no less difficult to deal with because coaches often must spend a lot of time convincing clients that they can help them. Skeptics ask a million questions before they'll buy in to the process: "How is this going to work?" and "How do I know this will help me improve my performance, become a better leader, deliver better results?"

Curiosity

Curiosity is similar to but different from skepticism. Although people with either may ask many questions, curious people are much more open to coaching. Many times, they haven't been exposed to coaching in the past and just need more information before they'll make a commitment.

Enthusiasm

Obviously, enthusiastic people are the easiest to coach and the most fun to work with. Their positive reaction is a direct result of the complexity of their workplace and marketplace and the rising demands for results. They believe in the principles of coaching because they think they make sense. The only negative here is that some people are overly enthusiastic — to the point that their expectations become unrealistic. They either believe that your coaching efforts will instantly transform them into a great leader or that they don't have to do much to make the process work for them. (See Exhibit 6.2 for a summary of reactions.)

Readiness Factors

Openness to New Experiences

This trait has nothing to do with intelligence. We've worked with very bright people who have absolutely refused to try any of the new things associated with Action Coaching. Other people simply aren't threatened by things that are new and different; they're energized and challenged when asked to look at themselves and

Exhibit 6.2. The Range of Reactions to Coaching.

Open				Closed
Enthusiasm	Curiosity	Skepticism	Denial	Concern or Fear
Understands the need to adapt to changing workplace; may have overly ambitious expectations.	Asks many questions; open but needs more information.	Needs convincing before buying into process; needs answers to questions.	Denies anything is wrong; may blame others; gets defensive; is offended by coaching.	Sees coaching as a black mark or punishment; is afraid of what it means; needs reassurance — coach must build trust.

their work from fresh perspectives. These people are good coaching clients.

Self-Awareness

We've found that people who are naturally introspective and have a good sense of who they are in both their personal and professional lives usually respond well to coaching. Conversely, people who give relatively little thought to who they are and their impact on others often struggle with coaching and make slow progress. You can tell this latter group just by how oblivious they seem to their impact on others; feedback tells you they're affecting people one way, and they're telling you they don't see this at all. Self-awareness is a key component of emotional intelligence.

Achievement Orientation

By achievement, we mean people who want to "be the best they can be." Coaching is ideally suited for people who want to break boundaries, set records, and push themselves in a variety of ways. Managers who want to maximize their potential as leaders and as human beings flourish in this process. People who aren't goal setters and aren't driven to achieve may experience difficulty.

Learning Orientation

We always encounter successful managers who think they've learned all there is to learn. They feel as though their expertise in one area somehow transfers to areas that they know little or nothing about. As a result, they act as if coaching is irrelevant to them; they've been there and done that and can't possibly benefit from any new experiences. This is as opposed to continuous learners — people who recognize that there is always more to learn. Continuous learners are highly coachable and respond well to the feedback and other forms of new information that are integral to the process. See Exhibit 6.3 for a checklist to help you determine your client's readiness for coaching. A second checklist helps you determine your own readiness.

Exhibit 6.3. How Ready Is Your Client? How Ready Are You?

To what degree is your client:	Low				High
1. Open to new experiences?	1	2	3	4	5
2. Energized by challenges and open to trying new things?	1	2	3	4	5
3. Self-aware?	1	2	3	4	5
4. Naturally introspective?	1	2	3	4	5
5. Interested in how others perceive him or her?	1	2	3	4	5
6. Action-oriented?	1	2	3	4	5
7. Focused on maximizing his or her potential?	1	2	3	4	5
8. A goal setter, driven to constantly improve?	1	2	3	4	5
9. Committed to continuously learning?	1	2	3	4	5
10. Interested in new information and ideas?	1	2	3	4	5

To what degree would you rate yourself as	Low				High
1. Open to new experiences?	1	2	3	4	5
2. Energized by challenges and open to trying new things?	1	2	3	4	5
3. Self-aware?	1	2	3	4	5
4. Naturally introspective?	1	2	3	4	5
5. Interested in how others perceive you?	1	2	3	4	5
6. Action-oriented?	1	2	3	4	5
7. Focused on maximizing your potential?	1	2	3	4	5
8. A goal setter, driven to constantly improve?	1	2	3	4	5
9. Committed to continuously learning?	1	2	3	4	5
10. Interested in new information and ideas?	1	2	3	4	5

Antiresistance Steps

Although some of the people we've coached have had an ideal mix of readiness factors and reacted positively to the idea of Action Coaching, many have offered resistance of one type or another. Whether it's a lack of self-awareness or a skeptical reaction about Action Coaching's potential benefits, people frequently enter the process with a certain level of resistance.

We've found that you can reduce or even eliminate that resistance by launching the process with the following five principles guiding your interactions:

First, *create a supportive environment*. This might seem obvious, but if you think about how a traditional sports coach interacts with his players, you'll understand that coaches don't naturally demonstrate empathy, listen carefully, or understand the challenges facing clients. You're going to ask people to take risks and confront their demons in certain instances, and you need to establish an environment in which they feel comfortable doing so. You can create this environment by

> *Reserving judgment.* Don't make the client feel she has been accused of a crime or has failed in any way until you're sure exactly what the issues are.
>
> *Communicating that you hear what the client is saying.* Don't sit there like a lump on a log or make perfunctory comments; give feedback that demonstrates that you've heard what she said and you appreciate her position (which doesn't mean you necessarily agree with it).
>
> *Establishing a warmly neutral tone.* Even if you're coaching someone who is your direct report, you shouldn't act like a boss or manager when you're dealing with him. If you do, you'll put the person you're coaching on guard. This doesn't mean you should be buddy-buddy either. What you should shoot for is a caring interaction, one in which you demonstrate that you have your client's interests at heart.

Second, *keep one eye on business results and the other on personal development and change*. You will encounter people who view any type of coaching as thinly disguised psychotherapy, and they don't believe therapy has any place or purpose in business. You need to allay these concerns by maintaining a focus on business results. Even as you're helping people develop and change, you need to keep linking this change and development to business issues by projecting how self-awareness, performance improvement, performance breakthrough, or transformation will achieve a significant business goal. Create a vision of the desired future for your client; give him a dramatic sense of how both he and the business will benefit.

Third, *adapt to the client's needs rather than have the client adapt to yours*. Some coaches impose certain behaviors and goals on clients. You need to be more flexible; adapt the process to the client's agenda and connect it with the organizational agenda for that client. Many people resist coaching because they feel like the company is making them do things they don't want to do. By allowing them to address their own needs, you obtain a buy-in to the process initially and have the freedom to move the process in organizational directions later on. The key here is to ask the person you're coaching point blank if he feels that something is being imposed on him; get the issue out in the open and talk about it. If your client does feel this way, explore different options that will alleviate this feeling while still moving him in a direction that will benefit the business.

Fourth, *favor practice over theory*. Certainly theory has a place in the way we approach coaching; it's useful in explaining why people act the way they do. But an overreliance on theory can alienate people. As they listen to a coach expound on conceptual frameworks or best practice ideas, their eyes glaze over and they think (or say), "You don't understand the constraints I'm operating under." Therefore, adjust your approach so that it works for a specific individual in a specific situation. Be realistic about what's possible rather than talk about what should be possible but isn't.

To melt resistance in this area, be pragmatic and concrete; be alert during discussions with clients for times when you're out of touch with his reality; make an effort to determine whether you really are out of touch or whether the problem resides with your client's perceptions.

Fifth, *establish clear boundaries*. Some of our coaching clients are quite concerned about self-disclosure issues: how much they have to disclose about themselves, what information will be shared with their boss and organization, what information can be considered off the record, and so on.

To avoid resistance over this issue, you need to lay out and discuss the ground rules from the start. This avoids questions about what's confidential and what other people need to know. The checklist in Exhibit 6.4 will help you get started dealing with resistance.

Exhibit 6.4. Antiresistance Checklist.

Item	Completed
1. Create a supportive environment.	❏
• Don't rush to judgment.	❏
• Communicate that you hear what the person is saying.	❏
2. Establish a warmly neutral tone.	❏
• Keep one eye on business results, the other on personal development.	❏
• Project how goal accomplishment will benefit the person.	❏
3. Adapt to the person's needs.	❏
• Ask if the person feels imposed on by the coaching.	❏
• Explore options to alleviate this concern.	❏
4. Favor practice over theory.	❏
• Be pragmatic and concrete.	❏
5. Establish clear boundaries.	❏
• Discuss ground rules from the start.	❏

The First Meeting: Getting Coaching
Off to a Good Start

Like many people who had made it in the highly competitive banking industry, Grace was tough. Having cut her teeth on the sales
and trading floor, she'd moved up because she'd achieved outstanding financial results. But as she moved up, her short fuse
and shorter attention span became more noticeable and more of a
handicap. We were told that management thought Grace had great
leadership potential and that there was an opportunity for her to
contribute more to the company in a leadership role but that her
temper and lack of focus were obstacles to her development.

When we were brought in to coach her past these obstacles, she
gave us a hard look and asked, "What is this coaching really all
about?" It was clear from the beginning that Grace had no interest
in expanding her self-awareness. She was as skeptical of the process
as anyone could be, and she wasn't shy about voicing her doubts.

At the same time, Grace clearly communicated to us that she
was very interested in furthering her career at the bank and wanted
to become more of a leader. We didn't start off the discussion explaining that brusqueness, a short-term mind-set, and a foul temper
were not necessarily hallmarks of leadership. Instead, we decreased
her resistance by employing a number of the techniques discussed
earlier. First and foremost, we created a supportive environment.
We didn't talk about her temper and short attention span as detri-
mental behaviors that had to cease immediately or she would never
be selected for a leadership position. Instead, we gently probed with
her why she sometimes lost her temper, listening patiently as she
rationalized her behavior and relating stories of other hot-tempered
executives and how their behaviors affected others. Grace notice-
ably relaxed after we made it clear that we were reserving judgment
and were eager to explore issues objectively.

Just as important, at the end of that first session we shared our
initial impression that Grace didn't have to make a major transfor-

mation to achieve what she and the company wanted—that what was required was self-awareness and performance improvement. We suggested ways in which that improvement might come about and described how, if she made the improvements we envisioned, she might have a better shot at a leadership position she coveted (this was a position that we had been told by management they wanted Grace to take on).

In that first session, Grace went from being a person who was highly skeptical about coaching to one who was moderately enthusiastic about seeing where the process might take her.

First-Meeting Checklist

When you meet with a client for the first time, you'll be tempted to move forward quickly, setting up goals, giving feedback, role-playing, and engaging in other process activities. You may be able to move forward quickly, but a great deal depends on the individual client and her situation. During and after the first meeting, use the following 7-point checklist to take a reading of your client's willingness and ability to move forward:

1. *Factor your client's specific traits into your opening approach.* If the person is highly self-aware, use that self-awareness as an entry point for a discussion of Action Coaching goals. If the person is a continuous learner, talk about what he or she would like to learn from the process.

2. *Try and read your client's reaction to coaching.* We've noted six common reactions from fear to enthusiasm, but there are certainly other possibilities; an individual may even have a mix of different reactions. The key is to figure out the predominant one and adapt your approach to address the client's specific response. You may be able to accelerate the process, given an enthusiastic response, or slow it down given denial or fear.

3. *Identify the real (as opposed to the purported) reasons for your client's problems or development issues.* Keep an open mind. This may

be difficult if you're coaching a direct report or peer and you have been involved with the issues and people; your biases may creep into your coaching. As much as you can, push these biases aside and relate to your client differently from the way you would in a typical work situation; make an effort during the first coaching meeting to understand why your client does what he does.

4. *Find out whether your client really understands how the organization hopes his behavioral changes will meet the organization's needs.* Be explicit about why you or the organization chose him to be coached. People falsely assume that coaching is a form of punishment or that it's a way to make people conform. Once people can connect the desired behavioral changes with larger business goals, they become more enthusiastic about the process. You might find that helping Joe become more visionary in his thinking or helping Joan become more innovative are nice goals, but they're not the real reason they're not achieving the results the organization wants. Explore what your client feels the obstacles to results are, and focus your work on these behaviors and attitudes rather than the ones assumed to be the problem.

5. *Address resistance rather than ignore it and hope it will go away.* Use our five antiresistance steps discussed earlier to deal with the issues that people talk about and the ones that simmer just beneath the surface.

6. *Determine whether there's consensus about who your client is and what he needs.* Are you hearing different stories from different people about the skills he needs to develop, negative behaviors he needs to eliminate, or opportunities for growth he needs to pursue? If the stories are conflicting, you may need to do some investigation to determine what the situation really is.

7. *Figure out what the real impact of your client's behavior and attitude is.* Test your assumptions before you act on them. Although your client may seem insensitive at first glance, you may discover that his tough exterior masks an ability to understand and respond to other people's needs—exactly the quality needed for a manage-

Exhibit 6.5. First-Meeting Checklist.

When to Do It	What to Do	Completed
Before the Meeting	1. Factor what you know about your client's specific traits and readiness factors into your opening approach.	❏
During the Meeting	2. Try and read your client's reaction to Action Coaching.	❏
	3. Identify the real (as opposed to the purported) reasons for your client's problems or developmental issues.	❏
	4. Find out whether your client really understands how the organization hopes his or her behavioral changes will meet the organization's needs.	❏
	5. Address resistance rather than ignore it and hope it will go away.	❏
After the Meeting	6. Determine whether there's consensus about who your client is and what he or she needs.	❏
	7. Figure out what the real impact of your client's behavior and attitude is.	❏

ment position he's being considered for. Although some people may complain about your client's drill-sergeant exterior, others may praise his willingness to drop that pose when they really need someone to talk to. It may make sense to gather information from multiple sources before you meet with your client. The better you understand the impact of behaviors, the better able you'll be to communicate it to the client and develop an effective plan to deal with it. (See Exhibit 6.5 for a summary checklist.)

You'll be asking a lot of the people you're coaching. It's difficult enough for people who are highly receptive and enthusiastic to transform their behaviors and attitudes or develop their capabilities in ways that benefit the organization. If you can launch the process on solid ground, you're that much better prepared to deal effectively with the various problems, obstacles, and distractions that will emerge later on.

Still, there is no such thing as problem-free coaching. When you're attempting to coach with one eye on the individual and the other on the business, you can expect that at some point your coaching strategy will go awry. The next chapter will help you deal with that eventuality.

7

Troubleshooting

We'd like to focus on three ways you might find yourself in coaching trouble and need advice: (1) assessing whether someone is uncoachable, (2) shifting coaching directions, and (3) helping someone acquire a key missing ingredient.

Let's start with the first area. Although most people are coachable, a significant percentage may *seem* uncoachable. They or their situations are extremely frustrating to deal with and cause coaches to wonder what in the world they can do to help them. At times, it may seem that a person will never change in any significant way or in a way the business needs to see change. At these times, it's important to understand why you've hit the wall in your coaching. If you know why a person isn't responding to the process, you can often work at removing the obstacles. Or if the obstacle is significantly large and unmoveable, it may be time to call it quits.

If you're coaching a person and asking her to change in a way that affects deep-rooted personality issues or attitudes, it may appear as if she's uncoachable because of the degree of difficulty. In these instances, coaches need to be patient and recognize that the transformation being sought isn't going to happen overnight. If, however, you're only asking someone to change surface-level behavior—for example, to learn to network or give more effective presentations—you probably won't encounter many uncoachable-seeming people.

Clients also appear uncoachable when they deny a problem exists or when they are unable to see what's wrong. We're working with a CEO now who doesn't realize that he keeps people apart. In an organization striving to create synergy between business units, this is a big problem. This CEO, however, is oblivious to his inability to bring teams together. As a result, trying to get him to change is frustrating because he perceives that he's already made the changes the organization needs him to make.

It's worth noting that people who are completely unaware of their problematic behaviors often are top executives or are in charge of tasks that have a huge impact on business goals. Because of their authority and impact, there's a desperate need for them to change, which is why a call goes out for a coach to intervene. But because of their power, other people's fear of giving them honest feedback, or their history of success, they may deny that they have a problem. They've achieved great results behaving one way, so they assume that if it worked before it will work again.

Again, the key here is to be patient and not jump the gun on declaring such people uncoachable. Feedback is a great tool for breaking through denial. If enough voices say the same things, the feedback has sufficient weight to make continued denial difficult.

Uncoachable Individuals: Eight Difficult Situations

The following eight situations are very common and can drive coaches to distraction. Either something inside the person being coached or in the environment makes him resistant to the coaching process. Sometimes, because these situations are so difficult, it's best to jettison clients from the process. At the same time, it may be a mistake to write them off prematurely. Consider the causes of their seeming uncoachability and follow our suggestions for trying to get them back on track.

The Rehabilitation Assignment

People are often funneled into coaching because they're performing poorly and a boss doesn't want to fire them or discipline them in any way. It may be that these individuals are uncoachable, at least in the sense that they lack the inner resources (a given skill or temperament) that a job demands. The organization expects you to rehabilitate them in the same way a jail is expected to rehabilitate a criminal—recidivism is likely in both cases, even if you manage to make some progress.

The key here is to determine whether the performance goal is realistic, given an individual's capacities. In some cases, the person may simply need training to reach this performance goal. Many times, however, the person will never reach it without a significant amount of time and experience. And some people will never reach it, given who they are and what they're being asked to do.

Quick-Fixers

The quick-fix mentality is extraordinarily frustrating for coaches and is all too common. People enter the coaching process and demand to be fixed; they want the answer to their performance problems immediately. If coaching came in a pill they could take once a day, they'd be much happier. What's uncoachable in these types of people is that they refuse to become engaged in the process. They don't understand that they need to evolve and adapt and that they have to make an emotional commitment rather than just an intellectual one to bring about personal change.

Quick-fixers can be coached if they're willing to make this commitment, but coaches need to push them to drop their "how long is this going to take?" attitude.

Conspiracies of Silence

This situation is maddening for coaches who know something is wrong but can't get anyone to admit it. Typically, an executive will enter the coaching process and insist it's a mystery to him why he's unable to meet the organization's goal for him. Not only that, but the people who work with and for him will also agree that it's a mystery to them. One of our clients, for instance, possessed a tremendous need to be right all the time. We determined by example and anecdote that he had to have the last word in every discussion and it had caused his people to stop challenging him. When we confronted him on this issue, he said, "How come I've never heard this from anyone before?" This conspiracy of silence happens all the time. When executives receive anonymous feedback, they often hear about their flaws. But when that executive attempts to discuss the feedback directly with his direct reports, they can deny that a stated flaw is a flaw and end up saying in so many words, "Oh no, not you boss. I don't know why anyone would say that."

This collusion between the client and his surrounding people can be a big problem, and the only way to surmount it is by exposing it for what it is. Sometimes you can obtain feedback "for the record" so that it's impossible for a client to deny problematic behaviors. Other times you may need to be more creative.

Stylistic Differences

A person's operating style may be completely at odds with a situation's requirements. For instance, a person who is classified as an introvert on the Myers-Briggs Type Indicator may have a terrible time in situations that call for him to be more extroverted. Coaches don't do personality transplants, and it's important to recognize when the organization is essentially asking you to achieve this impossible goal. But when stylistic differences exist, that doesn't mean the person is uncoachable. Action Coaching routinely encourages clients to moderate their natural preferences to meet important objectives. You can help the introvert learn to be more outgoing and effective in social situations by using the tools of the process. What you can't do is change an introvert into an extrovert.

Unmotivated People

If you're coaching a person who just doesn't care, all the tools of Action Coaching won't mean a thing. If a client is counting the days until retirement or is burned out, she may be uncoachable. As one client said to us, "Look, I'm old and I'm rich. Tell me again why this should matter to me." Similarly, high-achievers can be unmotivated because they feel they have few challenges left and nothing more to prove.

As much as you would hate to lose a high-achiever's talent, your role as a coach may be to advise your client to move on. If he can't fulfill the organization's mandate, it may be that he's figuratively uncoachable. In another environment, he may be highly coachable. As we've emphasized earlier, coaches must identify what motivates a client and use it to close the gap between who that person is and what the organization hopes he will be. But some people—because they're near the end of their careers or because they're unchallenged—have no identifiable motivation. In these cases, there's not much a coach can do.

Organization-Individual Disconnect

The organization's goal is that all managers become great developers of people, but when push comes to shove the organization doesn't support this goal. No one is rewarded for being a good developer of people. No one is selected for people development skills. We've met with clients and said, "This is the game and why we're here." They've responded, "This is the real game and here's how it's really played." When clients understand that the organization doesn't mean what it says, coaches are hamstrung.

About all you can do in these situations is focus on an individual's intrinsic motivation. What does a client really care about?

Where does he want to go in his career? It may be that becoming a good developer of people will serve him well wherever he goes, and it's in his best interests to acquire this skill.

Paralyzing Fear

Sometimes clients realize that coaching is their last chance. Whether or not this is true, it's their perception, and this perception creates such anxiety that they're unable to deal with the Action Coaching process. Other people simply are scared of doing anything new or different. At AT&T, many employees joined the company years ago, searching for the safety and security of being in a monolith; they weren't interested in a wild ride. AT&T now needs its people to take significant risks, and many of the veterans aren't up to it. Managers who are fearful, anxious, or risk-averse may have tremendous difficulty with Action Coaching because they lack the gumption necessary to try new things and take risks— requirements of our coaching process.

One of the most effective ways to help people get past these fears and become coachable involves transforming negative into positive energy. The negative valence—fear, anxiety, doubt—can be turned into the positive valence—enthusiasm, excitement, commitment. Catastrophizing helps accomplish this transformation. In a variety of ways, we get clients to reflect on the "worst that can happen." By encouraging them to articulate their worst fears, they can learn to reduce the terror they feel. Another piece of related advice: don't assume that fear always manifests itself by physical trembling or meek and mild mannerisms. Fearful people also shut down, withdraw, or strive for perfection. These people are just as uncoachable as those who have more traditional, fearful reactions. Again, the solution is to get them to verbalize their fears.

Distraction

What do you do when you discover that your client is having difficulties meeting organizational goals because he just got divorced, a loved one died, or some other personal matter has distracted him from the job at hand? At first glance, you may deem someone uncoachable because he seems utterly unable to focus. When you sit and talk with him, his mind appears to be elsewhere; you can't believe he'll ever be able to get past what's happening in his personal life and make an emotional commitment to coaching goals. We've found that you can't ignore these issues. Pretending they don't exist and hoping someone will snap out of it is a pipe dream.

At the very beginning, you need to help your client formulate a strategy to deal with these personal issues—finding a therapist, joining a support group, and so on. What really needs to happen is for your client to redirect his energy away from his personal problems and toward the coaching framework you're setting up. See Exhibit 7.1 for a summary of difficult situations and how to handle them.

Exhibit 7.1. Eight Difficult Situations and How to Handle Them.

Difficult Situation	Description	How to Handle
Rehabilitation assignment	Lacks inner resources	Determine whether the performance goal is realistic
Quick fixers	Won't engage in the process	Push client to own the problem.
Conspiracies of silence	No one will admit the problem—others are colluding	Expose the collusion; obtain other sources of feedback.
Stylistic differences	"Personality transplant" is needed	Encourage client to modify natural preferences.
Unmotivated client	Client just doesn't care	Consider advising client to move on.

(continued on next page)

Exhibit 7.1. (*continued*)

Difficult Situation	Description	How to Handle
Organization-individual disconnect	Organization doesn't mean what it says regarding people's goals in coaching	Focus on the individual's intrinsic motivation.
Paralyzing fear	Too anxious to try new things	Transform the negative energy into positive energy.
Distraction	Personal issue is taking the person's attention	Help client formulate a strategy to deal with the personal issue.

How to Handle the Unexpected and Shift Directions Accordingly

Action Coaching is a process of discovery, so you need to be willing to adapt your approach according to what you discover. The formal process we've outlined is fine as a starting point, but you may find it advisable to skip steps or change direction based on what you learn. It may be that the organization has one goal for your client when you begin, but you may learn enough about your client to determine that the goal has to be modified in some way—along with your strategy.

For instance, we were coaching a CEO of a Fortune 100 company as part of a larger coaching effort in his company. Human resources' goal for the CEO was modest; they really just wanted him to participate in 360-degree feedback as a symbolic gesture, demonstrating that he was behind the coaching program. When we met with him, however, we shared his 360-degree feedback with him and he was intrigued. He requested that we talk to his direct reports and get more feedback. As we worked with him, he became fascinated with the process and was eager for us to help him become a more effective leader of the company.

Certainly this was a relatively easy shift to make because it was endorsed by the CEO and the direction was clear. Sometimes, however, coaches don't realize that a shift has taken place or don't know what to do about it. Most of us prefer having things go according to plan, and most of us become confused when things go off track. To help you recognize when it's time to shift strategy, here are some questions you should ask yourself:

- *Is the original mission or purpose for coaching still valid or does it need to be modified?* Sometimes you don't know where an individual really is in her work life until you meet with her. On more than one occasion, we were shocked to discover that a person touted as a high-achiever was actually retired in place. If the original mission was to help her take on more responsibility, then you're going to be out of luck; her mind-set is such that she's no longer responsible for the work she has. There are also times when the organization changes direction and its needs for its employees change as well.

- *Is the relationship with your client effective?* Is there "chemistry" or a strong connection with your client? In some coaching relationships, there's not much of a connection. A certain distance is maintained (often at the behest of the coach), and the relationship is business-like and professional. Coaching relationships are professional, but there also should be an essential emotional connection. A level of trust is established. There's genuine respect and understanding between client and coach. This allows an openness and honesty that's critical for major performance improvements and transformation. If you find that the relationship isn't working—if there's no sense of trust or communication—then you may want to suggest that another coach take your place.

- *Are the techniques and tools you're using making a difference?* Sometimes you have to change these techniques and tools because they've become inappropriate or ineffective. A senior executive in an Action Coaching program was supposed to complete a developmental plan as the culmination of the coaching process. In accordance with the wishes of his company's HR department, we were using a developmental planning tool. This senior executive, however, disdained this type of tool. It became clear that he would create a much better developmental plan for himself if he weren't locked into the requirements of this tool and that he needed the freedom to explore different options on his own. Coaches must avoid falling in love with specific tools and techniques. Although they may be great for some people, they won't necessarily work for others, and when they don't, the coach needs to shift gears.

• *Should you bring other people into the coaching process?* Perhaps a better way to state this question is: Should the client's boss be brought into the process? Typically, bosses determine that their people need to be coached because of some problematic behavior, developmental need, or growth opportunity. What they sometimes fail to realize is that they're part of the problem; they need to see how they've contributed to the person's behavior or how they've failed to do everything that's necessary to encourage new behaviors. Coaches become stuck because they're focusing exclusively on their client and the client isn't the sole source of the problem. Bringing the boss into the process can have a catalyzing effect; it can change the dynamic of the interaction between client and coach and supply the missing puzzle piece.

We had one client who was assigned to manage a recently acquired company and relocated to the new division. His boss was dismayed at his management after a few months, claiming that he had "gone native"—that he was taking the acquired company's side on issues and failing to bring them into the fold with sufficient speed. Working with this client, we soon discovered that he was between a rock and a hard place, trying to gain the confidence of those who worked for the acquired company while helping merge cultures, policies, and practices. It was a difficult, lonely role, and it was one in which he received little support or encouragement from his boss. As a result, we shifted our approach to include the boss and help him see how he was making a difficult situation worse. Once the boss began to understand this, we found a way for our client to change his behaviors in a way that made him more effec-

tive and satisfied his boss. (We'll talk in greater detail about this issue in the next chapter.)

• *Are there signs of progress?* Coaches need to be alert to how
the process is affecting a client's attitudes and behaviors. Typical
signs that a client is making progress include experimenting with
new behaviors, implementing suggestions offered by the coach, and
receiving positive feedback from others about how a client has
changed or done something differently. If these signs aren't apparent, coaches need to shift their approach. We've found that one
common and effective shift is from nice coach to tough coach. If
being supportive, offering guidance, and acting as a sounding board
doesn't result in signs of progress, it may be time to become more
confrontational or to directly report the frustration, anger, and
other negative emotions your client is causing. One particularly
effective technique in this regard is "calling attention to the moment." Rather than referring to some incident in the past, coaches
should focus attention on a behavior that occurs when they're
meeting with clients. If the client has been accused of being a poor
listener, for instance, note how his attention wanders as you're
speaking. Dealing with real-time data is more uncomfortable than
data from the past, and this discomfort can rejuvenate the process.

• *Has something occurred outside the organization that renders
your coaching strategy obsolete?* More so than ever before, business
situations change rapidly. A company may want its people coached
so they can operate effectively on a global basis as they expand. A
downturn, however, may cause them to place less of a priority on
global requirements and more of a priority on cost-control and domestic markets. Sometimes, coaches miss the business shift because
they aren't paying attention to larger company and strategic issues.
They divorce themselves from anything that doesn't have a direct
impact on the goal for the client. Too late, they realize they've
helped their client change in ways that may no longer be relevant
to the new CEO, new owners, or new strategy. What they should
do is meet with their sponsor (or whoever brought them in to

coach) and talk about the environmental changes and how they affect what they're working on with a client.

- *Are you getting unintended results?* Perhaps we should rephrase this. Coaching, unlike training, always produces some unexpected reactions. But are your clients exhibiting new behaviors that they think are positive but that you or the company believe are negative? For instance, we coached a manager and shared feedback indicating that he had poor listening skills and communicated poorly. Almost immediately, he executed a 180-degree change. He was so intent on achieving a performance breakthrough that he began listening intently when he met with his direct reports. Rather than dominating the conversation, he remained unusually quiet except for a few highly specific comments. His direct reports freaked out; they distrusted his eerie silences; they assumed he was displeased with them. Part of the problem was that he had changed so quickly. When rapid change is introduced in a steady-state system, all sorts of odd things happen. If you're finding this happening with a client, slow things down. Emphasize the concept of trying out new behaviors, testing them slowly, obtaining feedback, and adjusting the behaviors if necessary. Be a talking partner for your client, giving him a sense of the behaviors that are working and those that aren't. Help him understand that he can't solve his problems in a day and that the solution needs to evolve.

- *Are you exposing issues you're unqualified or unable to handle?* We coached a marketing executive who was highly volatile and experienced wild mood swings. After one or two meetings with him, we suspected substance abuse. Rather than attempt to handle it alone, we brought in other, more specialized professionals to work with us. In another situation, we began receiving feedback indicating that our client might be guilty of sexual harassment. Again, we stopped the process and brought in others to investigate the allegations. As effective as coaching is, it's not a panacea for everything that ails your clients. Even though the process might help drug abusers or individuals with severe depression, neurotic behaviors, or racist tendencies—and even though their issues may be connected to their negative behaviors at work—it's important to acknowledge when you're out of your depth or out of the area you want to work in.

Missing Ingredients

Coaches often find that their clients are missing something that's crucial to the process. The missing piece may be internal (they lack self-awareness) or external (they lack organizational support for their development). For other types of training or coaching programs, these missing elements might not be crucial. But for Action Coaching, these are significant problems and can prevent a client from achieving the ambitious goals of performance improvement, breakthrough, or transformation.

Let's look at what you're likely to find missing and what you can do to compensate.

Lack of Focus on Individual Development

In many organizational cultures, managers are reluctant to admit that they need to learn new competencies or that they could use help in a certain area. There's a certain amount of hubris that goes with a prestigious organizational title, and many top managers are loathe to talk about their flaws and vulnerabilities. Without an organizational emphasis on managerial development, many executives enter coaching and resist any discussion or activity that exposes a weakness or need on their part.

• *Suggested action:* To counter that resistance, you might try benchmarking other companies where top executives went through coaching and were willing to admit their weaknesses and look at their developmental needs objectively. In our experience, top managers tend to listen to other top managers if they respect the other company. You might also locate someone within your own organization—preferably a top executive—who has either gone through the coaching process or is open and honest about his vulnerabilities and learning requirements.

Lack of Time or Inclination for Reflection

You'll encounter clients who find reflection to be a foreign concept. They are "doing" so much they don't have the time or opportunity to "be." As a result, when you encourage them to reflect on their actions and meditate on who they are, they'll look at you as if you've asked them to levitate. These are the people who at your first session glance impatiently at their watches and ask, "How long is this going to take?"

- *Suggested action:* Give them something specific to reflect on and a specific way to reflect. Sometimes the problem is that managers aren't clear what they should be doing when you ask them to contemplate their goals and problems. Clearly communicate what you would like them to roll around in their minds. Give them ideas and options for thinking about things. The first time they reflect, tell them to close their eyes and spend only five minutes; the next time, ten minutes; the third time, fifteen minutes. Write out a sentence pertaining to their issue and have them focus all their attention on it. Emphasize that reflection is not a logical, step-by-step process and that they should allow thoughts to come naturally rather than consciously work through points 1, 2, and 3 of an issue.

Lack of Honest Feedback

Feedback is critical to our coaching framework, but you may find the feedback you're collecting is skewed toward the positive. We've touched on this issue earlier. People are reluctant to say anything negative about others they work with and especially those who are top managers. As a coach, this isn't always easy to discern. You may receive feedback that contains some mild criticisms, but they've been toned down for public consumption. Also confusing the issue are clients who tell you they want their people to take them on and be honest with them. They insist they tell everyone they enjoy mixing it up and debating issues. This may be true most of the time. But if someone with power is aloof, impatient, or questioning just once in response to negative feedback, it has a tremendous impact on other people. They're reluctant to be negative again.

- *Suggested action:* To encourage honest feedback, assure people you interview that their input will remain anonymous. You might even suggest they write their comments on a piece of paper and send them in so that even you don't know who the source is. It might even be worthwhile to have a top executive issue a memo reiterating the need to provide coaches with honest feedback and emphasizing that there won't be negative consequences for doing so.

Lack of Self-Awareness

One of the more discouraging discoveries coaches can make is that their client isn't aware of why he does what he does. You've probably known executives who rationalized their behavior in many ways, creating all sorts of reasons for their actions. The COO who occasionally yells at and belittles people rationalizes his actions by saying that he hates being that way, but it's the only way he can get people to take action. The manager who avoids confrontation maintains she's perfectly willing to go toe to toe with someone, it's just that she doesn't like "abusing that management tool." Sometimes the client isn't in denial; she just isn't aware of her style and how it affects others. Whatever the case, self-awareness is necessary for coaching to work. If you don't have a window of self-awareness, all the information you gather and all your tools won't penetrate.

- *Suggested action:* To create this window, you need to break through the denial or illuminate the shadow parts of people. In terms of the former, it can be useful to videotape their interactions with others, providing clear evidence of what they do. In terms of the latter, it helps to build a case based on direct feedback surveys and other materials demonstrating how their behaviors affect others. You frequently need to confront people with the facts—the consequences of their behaviors, the reasons they won't be able to handle increased responsibility unless they transform themselves, and so on. It may be that your client will become self-aware simply because he had a coach who communicates honestly and listens deeply. Other people, however, require direct confrontation or they'll never see themselves as they really are. You can try engaging in open dialogue first, but if that doesn't work, confrontation is necessary.

Lack of Support to Confront Issues

Our coaching plans often involve other members of the organization, and sometimes these other people fail to support the client's efforts to change. We have one client who has been moved from having regional responsibility to managing globally, and we were coaching him with the goal of getting him to take this larger view. Most of the people he used to work with, however, still have regional roles. As he tests new behaviors as a global manager, he's met with hostility from his former peers—they don't like the way he is intruding on their territory. He needs help from others to make this transition successfully, and he's not receiving it.

• *Suggested action:* Coaches need to work with their sponsors to educate others in the organization so that they understand what a client is going through and learn how to support his efforts to change. If you don't have a sponsor—if you're coaching peers or direct reports without formal sponsorship—you may have to use your own political and communication skills to generate the support you need from others. This isn't always as difficult as it sounds. We've found that others in the organization are threatened by coaching only when they don't understand what you're trying to do and how it will help the company; they assume that coaching will only help the individual. If you can persuasively make a case for organizational gains, you and your client will probably receive the support you require.

Lack of Skill

People enter coaching without key skills. Some of the more common missing skills include understanding and applying technology, understanding globalization and the impact of culture on market and consumer decisions, the impact of speed on product introduction, making innovation happen, and dealing with an entitled workforce.

- *Suggested action:* If this is the case, you may be able to build a skill-building component into the coaching process. Or you may have your client sign up for appropriate training sessions or workshops. You also need to be aware, however, that some people simply lack the capacity to master certain skills. If you suspect this is the case, it's advisable to stop the process immediately.

Lack of Depth

Sometimes you'll find you can't quite put your finger on what's wrong. A client just doesn't seem to grasp the change he needs to make or the problem with his attitude. It may seem clear to you but it's cloudy to him. What's confusing is that your client is smart as a whip, and he's been highly successful. Now, however, he's just stumped. The problem is that he hasn't had enough "wear on his treads." He hasn't failed at all or enough; he hasn't overcome career obstacles; he hasn't worked in a variety of situations; he hasn't dealt with stressful personal issues. As a result, he's only capable of looking at the business through a functional lens. Or he doesn't have the ability to be introspective. We're coaching the thirty-five–year-old founder of a successful start-up company, and even though he's brilliant, he just hasn't done or seen enough to recognize that the style that worked when he founded and grew the company isn't as effective now that the company's starting to mature. Although action coaching adds a certain amount of depth to people who go through it, it may not be enough—it hasn't been for this particular individual.

• *Suggested action:* Sometimes the only thing that will supply this missing ingredient is experience. You need to give someone time on the job before he assumes a larger role or before he's able to see things from a broader perspective. To accelerate this process, you may want to create a plan that exposes your client to jobs and situations that you believe will help season him. It may involve making sure your client spends some time in an office in a Third World country or having him become more involved with teams. You may also want to include mind-opening assignments as part of the plan, such as writing a vision statement, working in a volunteer shelter, or traveling to unlikely places.

Lack of Personal Commitment to Change and Growth

It's ironic that some of the most hard-charging, decisive managers who go through coaching are also the ones who are the most passive when it comes to dealing with their personal issues. "That's just the way I am" they respond, when told that a behavior or an attitude is preventing them from achieving organizational goals. What it often boils down to is that they lack the internal motivation to change. Coaches can't create that motivation using some artificial means. All they can do is provide the opportunity and environment in which it can emerge. Some people just aren't ready to bring this motivation to the surface, and if you're trying to coach someone like this, you probably should realize that he's not going to make a major transformation.

• *Suggested action:* Your role is simply to provide the support and structure to help a client find her motivation and make a commitment to change. Ideally, your work with a person will help her become more aware of why "being the way I am" is preventing her from achieving goals both she and the organization want her to achieve. If you can hold up a mirror through feedback, shadowing, and other tools and let her come to this realization, you may help her supply the motivation to change.

Lack of Context

Another way of stating this is that people need to see the big picture and their place in it. If a person only knows how to perform her
function or understands only what her team is supposed to do,
that's insufficient. She needs to develop a sense of how her individual actions relate to her boss, to other teams, to the company as
a whole, and to what the competition is doing. Leaders possess context; they can give others a sense of not only what they're doing but
why. People who enter coaching without this context are often
confused at first, floundering around trying to figure out why they
should change. Personal change makes much more sense when a
person can see how new behaviors might positively affect everyone
from direct reports to the business strategy.

• *Suggested action:* To help clients develop this context, it's
important to provide them with information and ask them questions that get them to develop a theory about why they do what
they do. One of the best things you can do in this regard is work
with them on creating strategies, visions, and missions for a team,
department, or even an organization. These exercises force people
who have rarely looked beyond their narrow roles to grapple with
big-picture issues. Hold your clients accountable for completing
this assignment thoughtfully and thoroughly. Make it clear that
you're not going to accept a cursory analysis or a thrown-together
strategy. You might even say that you're going to share their ideas
with someone in management to add significance to the assignment. See Exhibit 7.2 for a summary of how to compensate for
missing skills and characteristics.

In addition to all these missing ingredients, you may find that
one other thing is absent from the coaching process: your client's
boss. Involving the boss is crucial for coaching efficacy, and how and
when to involve this key person is something we'll look at next.

Exhibit 7.2. Missing Ingredients and How to Compensate.

What's Missing	How to Compensate
Organizational focus on development	Benchmark other organizations or executives who use coaching and are open to the need for development.
Time or inclination	Use reflection tools to spur action.
Honest feedback	Ensure feedback will be anonymous.
Self-awareness	Video- or audiotape the person's interactions with others.
Support to confront issues	Work with sponsors to educate others in the organization.
Skill	Offer skill building and training.
Depth	Create situations in which client can gain experience; give it time.
Personal commitment to change and growth	Help client find internal motivation.
Context	Provide information; help clients obtain information about organizational context.

8

Who's the Boss?

To generate performance breakthroughs or transformations in a way that dovetails with organizational needs, your client's boss must play a key role in the process. The boss often has great insight into how to link individual behaviors and organizational goals. The boss may also be in a position to facilitate new, desired behaviors—and, in fact, may be contributing to current behaviors that are impeding the client's progress. Integrating the boss into the process, however, can be tricky for a number of reasons. In a few cases, you may decide it's best to exclude that person.

To make this and other determinations, it's useful to understand the triangular boss-coach-client relationship. In some instances, you'll be playing two roles in this triangle. If you're coaching a direct report, you need to separate the boss part from the coach part and hold this relationship up to the light, considering it as objectively as possible. We want to make it clear that just because you are wearing both hats doesn't mean you will automatically factor in a boss's perspective. You need to make a conscious effort to do it, or that perspective may well take a back seat to your coaching role.

It's also possible that you're coaching a direct report at the behest of your boss, who, for example, may have been waiting patiently for Charlie to grow into a crucial role and it hasn't happened. Now the boss is out of patience and says you have to move Charlie up or out. Although your role relative to that of the boss may vary, what remains constant is the need to integrate the boss into the coaching process.

The Boss: Part Problem, Part Solution

More often than not, the boss is the one who sees the need for a coach. As a result, she expects regular reports about her direct report's progress. She may want specific details of what's being done and how quickly. Not only does this present confidentiality problems, it presents political ones as well. What if you discover that the boss is the source of many of the problems your client is experiencing—that the client is not fulfilling the mandate the organization has for him because the boss is so poor at providing support and direction?

In the ideal scenario, the coach limits interaction with the boss and encourages the boss and her direct report to communicate with each other. Rather than get caught in the middle and end up as a referee in a dispute, the coach should allow the boss and her direct report to learn to deal with each other effectively. Unfortunately, this isn't always possible. The situation may have deteriorated past the point where they can work together without intervention. Or it may be that the client is too intimidated by the boss. Or it's possible that the boss is uninterested in the process or just doesn't have the time to devote to it. Whatever the reason, you may need to work closely with your client's boss in many cases. In these situations, you should try and define for your client what information will remain confidential and what needs to be shared with the boss when you report to her. A trusting, open relationship between coach and client is crucial, and that relationship will crumble if the client believes the coach is sharing private information with the boss.

It's more of a challenge to maintain that trust when the boss views coaching as a last resort. Typically, executives find themselves in a quandary about whether to keep a person; it's a toss-up whether to invest more time and money in him or let him go. In one way, turning the coach into an "assessor" changes the dynamic of the process. In some instances, try reasserting the process, enlisting the boss in the effort to help her direct report change his behaviors in ways that result in significant performance improvement and achievement of business objectives.

Some bosses don't realize how integral they are to both the problem and the solution. They often assume that a direct report's problematic behavior has nothing to do with them. Or they believe that a person's need to develop in a certain direction is beyond their control. In the vast majority of cases, bosses can use their ability to promote, reward, say yes or no, compliment, criticize, support, or reject to influence their direct reports' behavior. A boss may help you solve the problem that prompted the call for a coach in the first place.

Authority Figures: Identifying How the Client Relates

Whatever clients' specific problems or goals might be, they frequently have something to do with authority issues. In the early self-awareness phase, explore how clients relate to people in power. Their attitudes often evolve from how they related as kids to authority figures such as parents and teachers. It's valuable to understand this dynamic and help clients relate to authority in more productive ways. The first step in doing so is determining which of the following two types best describe your client:

Pleasers

These people follow orders well and do a good job of meeting a boss's requirements for them. They seek approval and become upset and uncertain if a boss is displeased with anything they do or say. In one sense, pleasers fit the old definition of "organization men"; they blend in well and don't rock the boat. Even today, some bosses prefer pleasers over others because they do what they're told. Although pleasers are skilled at meeting requirements, they also lack what is required in many organizations today. Many times, organizational goals for managers call for a willingness to challenge authority and an ability to look beyond the conventional view.

Rebels

Either overtly or covertly, rebels resist authority. When resistance is overt, it manifests itself as constant arguing with the boss or even sabotage (going to the boss's boss with an appeal to reverse a decision, for instance). The covert expression of this rebellious attitude may be passive-aggressive behavior. In these cases, a manager may seem to agree with the boss but then carry out an assignment in a different way than the one agreed upon. This covert resistance can be terribly upsetting to a boss who thinks he's achieved consensus and moves a project forward, only to find that he was mistaken.

Expect clients to tell you things like, "I don't care what my boss thinks" or to say that the issue isn't relevant because their organization has been flattened and bosses in general are no longer of much importance. In reality, every organization is a political field where the dynamics of power and authority are always present. Although the traditional notion of "boss" may have changed and the structures may be different, most people still report to someone. Helping clients understand their attitudes about this boss is often a linchpin issue in coaching. Performance improvement, performance breakthrough, and transformation almost always involve a client's boss in some way. If your client doesn't realize how he relates to his boss — or if he's operating under false assumptions about this relationship — it will be difficult for him to make progress.

Evaluation Tools

Evaluate the relationship in terms of not only what clients' attitudes are but how bosses perceive their direct reports. Who needs to change, and what does each person need to do in order to develop in ways that line up with business strategy?

It's usually wise to obtain feedback directly and indirectly from the boss at the outset of coaching. Rather than rely on one source, collect different types of information about how a boss views your client. Indirectly, you can gain valuable information by looking at various performance reviews, as well as other written comments by the boss about your client. Depending on the circumstances, consider using a survey or interviews of other people in your client's group to determine how peers see the situation. A more direct way is to interview the boss.

What you're searching for are answers to the following questions:

Are there certain behaviors that the boss finds counterproductive, irritating, or potentially harmful?

Are there specific incidents involving the client that support the boss's perspective?

Does the boss seem to be unfairly biased against the client in any way? Is the tension between them a result of personal differences, or is it related to performance issues?

Is there corroboration from other people (team members, HR, others) for the boss's perspective?

How would the boss like to see his direct report change? What specific behaviors or attitudes should be changed?

Would these changes be classified as self-awareness, performance improvement, performance breakthrough, or transformation?

Would these changes help the client achieve organizational goals?

How is the boss willing and able to support the changes that need to be made? Is the boss willing to make changes in the way he works with and relates to his direct report?

It's equally important to determine how clients want to relate to their bosses. In talking to clients and others about this issue, you want to keep the questions shown in Exhibit 8.1 in mind.

In many instances, answers to these questions involve a client's inability to tell the boss the truth. Many people are simply unable to level with the boss; they can't imagine being completely honest. Whether or not the perception is accurate, people often believe that bosses are too difficult, controlling, or insecure to tell them the truth. This avoidance of the truth is unacceptable. Whatever the organizational goal might be for a particular client, communicating ideas honestly and without shading is usually a key requirement for reaching that goal. Company after company is recognizing that the quality of information they possess and the richness of ideas they bring to bear on issues are important for gaining a competitive edge. In many organizations, however, ideas are watered down, and information is of uneven quality because people are afraid to be honest. In hierarchical organizations, people naturally protect themselves and their people, withholding innovative ideas or camouflaging bad news. As a result, even confident managers are afraid to talk straight with their boss or to suggest a risky idea.

Encourage your clients to explore what might happen if they told a boss the truth. Through role-playing and other tools, get clients to test the waters and realize that the truth usually does much more good than harm.

The Coach as Intermediary and Interpreter

It's difficult for people to be brutally honest with their bosses. Some bosses are vindictive and short-tempered; others are myopic in their self-perception and refuse to see other sides to themselves. It can be intimidating and frustrating to communicate directly and honestly with bosses who are like this. Fortunately, you're in a position to facilitate an exchange of information. Coaches are neutral; they work without bias or political baggage. Even if you're coaching a direct report, you should make a clear distinction

Exhibit 8.1. Boss-Employee Interview Questions.

Boss Questions	Employee (Client) Questions
Are there certain behaviors you find counterproductive, irritating, or potentially harmful in the employee?	What does the boss do or say that impedes your achievement of organizational goals?
What specific incidents involving the employee support this perspective?	Is your boss fair? Does your boss treat you the way everyone else is treated?
Is there tension between you and the employee as a result of performance? Is it more a result of personal differences?	Are there tension points in your relationship with your boss? What are disagreements or conflicts usually about?
What do other members of the team or department observe in the person's behavior?	Do you feel defensive, angry, dishonest, or uncertain when interacting with your boss? Do you have an example of how this occurs?
How would you like to see the employee change? What specific behaviors or attitudes would you like to see changed?	How would you like to see your boss change?
Would these changes be classified as self-awareness, performance improvement, performance breakthrough, or transformation?	What new behaviors on the part of the boss would facilitate your achievement of self-awareness, performance improvement, performance breakthrough, or transformation?
How would these changes help the employee achieve organizational goals?	
How are you willing and able to support the changes? Are you willing to make changes in the way you work with the employee?	

between how you relate to him as a coach versus as a manager. Schedule specific times for coaching; have your coaching interactions take place outside the usual places you meet so that it's clear the relationship is different.

The boss issue came up in our work with Dwight, the president of a Fortune 500 company. In most respects, Dwight is an outstanding leader. Not only is he people-oriented, but he relates well to employees at all levels and is extremely charismatic. What people don't like about Dwight and what they talk about bitterly behind his back is that he plays favorites. Dwight has his pets, and they seem to receive preferential treatment when it comes to promotions and choice assignments. This bias is very discouraging to people throughout the organization, dampening enthusiasm and initiative. The top managers in the company are well aware of Dwight's favoritism—to a certain extent, they are the beneficiaries of it—and they recognize that it is having a negative effective on morale and productivity. Although some of them have waltzed around the subject in informal conversations with Dwight, none have addressed the issue directly and clearly.

While coaching people who worked for Dwight, we met with him and identified the pattern we had discovered. At first, Dwight denied that he played favorites. It's fair to say that he was a bit upset at our suggestion. But after some discussion and after he reviewed some of the feedback we had received (the feedback was anonymous), Dwight was much more willing to consider that some of the company's problems he had blamed on his executives were actually a result of his own attitudes and policies. Dwight didn't automatically accept the idea that he played favorites, and he made valid points about how the people he "depended on" were the ones who were the most effective managers. Still, over time he became more aware of his tendency to favor a chosen few and the negative impact this had on morale. This didn't solve all the problems that needed to be addressed among his staff, but it did create an environment that was more conducive to problem solving.

The Boss-Obstacle Checklist

As a coach, there's nothing more frustrating than moving a client toward a breakthrough only to find that he's stuck at the brink because of his boss. Bosses can create all sorts of obstacles to coaching efficacy, and the following checklist will help you diagnose and deal with these obstacles:

- *Boss refuses to become involved or provide feedback.* We're working with a senior executive who complains that his boss doesn't make his expectations clear. We talked to the boss about this issue, and our client's boss explained that he would prefer to remain a "passive observer" because he believes his involvement would only impede the senior executive's progress. The boss is very humble and is convinced he has poor coaching skills. "I would just confuse him if I were to become involved," he said. What this boss fails to realize is that he can become an important part of the triangle of improvement—that his expectations can serve as a catalyst for that improvement far more powerfully than anything we say or do as coaches.

A lack of involvement can manifest itself as a refusal to provide feedback. The boss needs to level with the client, to provide specific information that serves as a catalyst for change. Although bosses often are willing to share this information with coaches, they are unwilling to do the same with their direct reports. Filtered through coaches, the feedback doesn't have the same impact. People need to hear it from the horse's mouth.

- *Boss doesn't believe in coaching.* In these instances, the only reason they're allowing a direct report to be coached is that top management has endorsed coaching or the boss's boss has brought you in. Their skepticism becomes an obstacle because they don't participate with any enthusiasm or creativity. They also communicate their skepticism to your client, which makes it difficult for him to take coaching seriously.

- *Boss views coaching as a last-ditch effort.* If the boss communicates that there's not much hope for the client or that this is a last-chance scenario, he'll rob you of a supportive environment that is conducive to change. "Is this outplacement counseling or coaching?" is an appropriate question to ask bosses. Communicate that coaching isn't designed to let people down more softly when they're about to be fired. If the boss doesn't believe coaching can create the performance improvement the company requires, she won't contribute much even if she is participating.

• *Boss's behavior is creating the very behaviors the boss wants the client to change.* We worked with a client whose boss was dogmatic, controlling, and punitive. Of course, he felt that his direct report would be far more effective if he became more assertive. The irony of this situation was lost on this boss. He didn't see how his personality was causing our client to act in ways he wanted changed. In cases such as this one, keep the boss out of the coaching process until later on, and only after you've worked out a more productive relationship agreement between the boss and your client should he be brought back in.

• *Boss is in trouble.* He's about to be fired or is in political hot water or has lost the support of his peers. Whatever the problem, coaching is difficult because it may be futile to involve the boss when he probably will not be your client's boss in the near future. It's also problematic because the boss can't marshal the required resources and isn't tied in to the larger organizational goals for your client.

• *Boss is at loggerheads with the client.* In these cases, the boss often calls in the coach to "fix" the client. There's often a history of problems between the two people, and there's a good deal of emotion and energy attached to these problems. None of this is particularly problematic if the boss really is willing to deal with the relationship issues and is interested in investing himself emotionally as well as intellectually in confronting the source of the conflict. Too often, however, bosses just want their direct reports fixed. They don't see themselves as part of the problem, and therefore they don't see themselves as part of the solution.

- *Boss is negative.* Performance improvements, breakthroughs, and transformations won't happen if the environment doesn't support change. Some bosses we've worked with rarely if ever say an encouraging word or provide any kind of positive incentives. They create a climate in which no matter what a coach does, people feel they can never win or excel.

- *Boss is looking for someone in his own image.* Just as some parents try to make their children be like them, some bosses insist that their direct reports be like them. We're working with a kind, soft-spoken manager who has an executive position with a large not-for-profit association. Respected by his peers and effective as a lobbyist and a fundraiser, this man is not living up to his boss's expectations for him; he hasn't developed in ways necessary to meet certain fundraising targets. She believes that if he were more assertive and forceful, he could raise more money and sway more lobbyists. Needless to say, she is tremendously assertive and forceful. As coaches, we can't agree with this woman's conclusion about her direct report. Our feeling is that if he were to assume his boss's powerful persona, he would be going against his nature. Even worse, our client has internalized the constant sniping of his boss over the years ("Why can't you call him again? What are you afraid of?") and now underestimates his capabilities; this is the real cause for his performance decline.

- *Boss is rule-oriented.* This type of boss makes it difficult to come to terms with performance issues. Typically, rule-obsessed people are unhappy with their direct report's performance, but they're measuring that performance based on how the tasks were done rather than on outcomes achieved. Although the boss may say that the client needs to make performance gains to meet organizational goals, what he really means is that the client has to learn to do things according to the boss's rules.

There aren't always easy ways to eliminate these obstacles, so you should begin by assessing how formidable they actually are.

Specifically, how important is the boss to your client's performance goals? Breakthroughs, for instance, require working with other departments, securing resources, and so on. Bosses are an integral part of this process. But transformations are much more focused on the individual. The boss can play an important role, but the systemic issues are less important than who an individual wants to become and what he's willing to risk to get there.

In organizations that have been flattened and have moved away from hierarchical structures, bosses have become less relevant to performance issues. It may be that a boss is only tangential to your client's issues for this reason. Personality also plays a role. Some people naturally are joined at the hip with their boss: they pay close attention to a boss's expectations, they have become skilled at managing authority, and they place great weight on how a boss perceives them. In these instances, don't ignore the boss or minimize his input.

What to Do When the Boss Plays a Pivotal Role

After you've identified the specific boss-obstacle, figure out how to deal with both your client and the boss in order to minimize or remove that obstacle. Just being aware of what the obstacle is can facilitate this process; you can clear up your client's misconceptions about the problem and also open a dialogue with the boss. Sometimes, however, this isn't enough. The issues go deeper for your client and the boss, and you need to use more sophisticated techniques to achieve positive results. Here are some techniques we've found to be effective:

• *Break unproductive patterns.* Many boss-client relationships are locked into predictable patterns, and clients are waiting and wishing for the boss to change. "If only the boss would communicate more, then I'd know what to do" or "If only the boss would provide me with more resources, then I could be more effective" are good examples of the if-only game many managers play. Don't let clients get away with playing this game. Challenge the client's basic assumption about his relationship by saying, "Let's assume the boss is not ever going to change, that he's always going to be like this until he retires. Knowing this, what are you going to do?" By shifting the focus away from what the client can't control (how the boss is) to things he can control (his own behaviors), you've given him a positive path for action.

- *Clarify what is needed from the boss.* Performance improvement or even a breakthrough may be sparked by formulating a clear agenda for the boss. Your client may have never spelled out what she needs from her boss to boost performance or what her expectations are. Does she need the boss to help her obtain specific resources? Does she want him to run interference? Does she wish that he would visit her customers? Work with your client to define this agenda for the boss—an agenda tied to meeting business objectives.

- *View the boss as a customer.* Some clients are terrific when it comes to anticipating customer needs but are abysmal when it comes to understanding their boss. This technique helps people disentangle themselves emotionally from the boss-employee relationship and allows them to think in terms they feel more comfortable with. Just talking about the boss as a customer helps some people perceive what needs to be done, as opposed to what they've been doing.

- *Put the client in the boss's shoes.* You'll find that some of your clients are so wrapped up in their own issues in working with the boss that they've failed to take the boss's issues into account. What we're suggesting here is that you help them build empathy and perspective by exploring the pressures the boss might be under and other factors that might be affecting his attitude and behavior. Seeing things from the boss's frame of reference can temper clients' anxieties and relax them enough that they can try new behaviors.

- *Role-play the boss.* Some people just aren't good at confronting, communicating, or negotiating with their boss. Sometimes they need to rehearse what they're going to say or how they're going to say it (to get what they want). Take the boss role down to gestures, expressions, and tone of voice. If a boss is evasive, act this way and see how your client responds. Again, this gives clients a chance to experiment with different approaches and find one that's effective. It also allows them to make communication, confrontation, and negotiation mistakes without negative consequences; they can learn from what they've done wrong and not repeat it.

• *Ask for feedback from the boss.* Sometimes this technique is in direct response to the boss who doesn't provide feedback, as described previously. Other times, however, the need for feedback is related to some other issue that's preventing a client from achieving his organizational mission. Encourage clients to solicit feedback first from peers, direct reports, and customers and then from the boss. This is a good approach if the client suspects the feedback he's going to receive from the boss is negative and that it doesn't jibe with the way other people view him. Obtaining feedback from others first isn't so that clients can use these data as a weapon during a confrontation with the boss—"See, other people don't think I'm lazy and uninspired"—but as a way of providing a realistic context both for the client and the boss.

• *Help clients own their truth.* Allow them to acknowledge what's really motivating their behaviors (behaviors the boss might view negatively or that would cause them to fall short of goals in the boss's eyes). Some people find it easier to blame the boss for their problems than to admit difficult truths; they may know the truth of a situation but they talk around it, never really allowing themselves to accept this truth as the central issue (they may think about it as tangential or secondary).

For example, Sam was recruited about a year ago from a West Coast company by an East Coast organization. A transition plan was put in place that would allow him to assume greater responsibility and take over some of the tasks of the top executive who hired him. Because his wife had a flourishing career on the West Coast, Sam left her and the kids there and moved East on his own;

the plan was to bring them out in a year or two, assuming the position worked out. During that first year, it did work out. In fact, in many respects it surpassed Sam's expectations. He was doing challenging work and learning a lot. At the same time, however, Sam's boss, the man who had recruited and hired him, was a "brilliant lunatic." As smart as he was, this boss was also mercurial and highly demanding. Contrary to his promise, he refused to designate Sam as his successor until Sam moved his wife and children to the East Coast. For months Sam was stuck in an awful limbo, feeling that his boss had misled him and wondering if the gamble of moving would result in his being designated the successor. Distracted and at times distraught, Sam was having trouble fulfilling his commitment to the company.

Sam's truth was that he was more committed to his family than he was to the organization. Once we helped him identify this truth and convinced him to talk about his concerns with his boss, Sam's performance improved, as did his relationship with the boss. Although this truth didn't guarantee Sam's future at the company, it did make the issues clearer for him. And he found it easier to work with his boss after owning his truth.

- *Teach clients active listening and coaching skills.* This is the opposite of passive listening, when a person filters what a boss is saying through her own anxieties, assumptions, and projections. And it's as opposed to confronting the boss or saying something in exactly the wrong way. Many people refute rather than absorb when they listen, and part of the active listening technique is encouraging clients to find areas of agreement and understanding while they listen rather than rush to their own defense. The coaching aspect of this technique is giving clients a sense of "teachable moments" in relationships and showing that there is a time, a place, and a style that will maximize a boss's receptivity to the information the client is trying to impart.

- *Distinguish between style and substance.* This is a confusing area for some managers, and this confusion can distract them from the task at hand. Each boss has a style, and it's useful to know what

that style is. Style inventories such as the Myers-Briggs Type Indicator or the CDR Leadership Risk Profile help identify that style
for clients. When people don't identify this style, they tend to
perceive irreconcilable differences between themselves and their
bosses. They complain bitterly about how their introverted boss
should communicate more with them. They get all hung up on this
fact and don't try to work around it. Recognize that bosses and direct reports with very different styles but with shared values can
work well together. Once clients see that they in fact do have common ground with their boss—that they both are committed to a
certain goal, for instance—then the style ceases to be an impedi-
ment. See Exhibit 8.2 for a summary of obstacles and how to overcome them.

The Balancing Act

You can expect to be placed in uncomfortable situations as part
of the boss-client-coach triangle, especially when the boss has
brought you in as a coach. We hear the following questions from
bosses all the time: Do you think he can change or is this the way
he is? Is she willing to change? Does she want to? Is she capable of
achieving more?

When you hear these questions, you're going to struggle with
how to answer them. On the one hand, there's the right-to-know
argument. If the boss brought you in as coach and your client's performance improvement is crucial to his group's success, then perhaps you owe him a certain amount of information. On the other
hand, your client probably wouldn't be open and honest with you if
he knew you were going to repeat everything he said to the boss.

Although each situation is different, you need to try and do
what is best for both the client and the organization simultane-
ously. Weigh the impact of the information you divulge on both
parties. Remember, what the boss is really asking is whether there's
hope: Can my direct report be resurrected? Can she become the
person we need her to become?

Exhibit 8.2. Boss Obstacles and How to Overcome Them.

Boss Obstacles		How to Overcome Them	
Boss refuses to become involved or provide feedback	Break unproductive pattern	⇧	Challenge client's assumptions and urge new action
Boss doesn't believe in coaching	Clarify what's needed from boss	⇧	Have client ask boss for what client needs
Boss views coaching as last-ditch effort	View boss as a customer	⇧	Shift client's view of relationship to minimize emotional charge
Boss is creating behaviors client needs to change	Put client in boss's shoes	⇧	Use role playing so client gains empathy and perspective
Boss is in trouble	Role-play the boss	⇧	Use role play to rehearse difficult discussions
Boss and client are at loggerheads	Ask for feedback	⇧	Gain peer-client feedback and compare with boss feedback for discrepancies
Boss is negative	Help clients own their truth	⇧	Help clients clarify their view of the situation and own it
Boss is looking for someone in his or her own image	Teach clients active listening and coaching skills	⇧	Help clients listen with an open mind and confront problems
Boss is rule-oriented	Distinguish between style and substance	⇧	Use style instruments to understand boss-client dynamics

To a certain extent, you can answer these questions to the boss's satisfaction and maintain confidentiality by identifying where the problem lies. It may be the client's attitude, boss-client miscommunication, or any number of general factors. For instance, by explaining to the boss that the problem is a skill deficiency and detailing the steps that might remedy it, you usually get at the heart of the boss's concern. You can then avoid the client's bitter complaint that he's told the boss he needs training in this area and that the boss refused to grant the request.

Perhaps the best way to handle this delicate situation, however, is to help the boss assume the role of partner in coaching rather than of intruder or observer. When a boss says, "What can I do to help us achieve our goals for Joe," you can set parameters for his participation in coaching that don't violate anyone's confidences and meet the company's agenda for your client.

The yin-yang in relationships with bosses is conflict-collaboration. Some conflict is always going to exist; some collaboration is essential despite this conflict. You can expect to coach people who are having difficulty with these two issues, not only as they relate to bosses but within the gestalt of all types of work relationships. As you'll see, coaching people so they strike the right balance between conflict and collaboration is necessary to achieve individual and organizational goals.

Part IV

Coaching to Change Your Company

9

Encouraging Productive Collaboration and Constructive Conflict

Here and in the following chapters, we'll concentrate on some of the most common issues you'll face as a coach. Whether you're a manager informally coaching your direct reports or you have a formal coaching role in your organization, you're bound to encounter certain types of vexing problems and situations.

For instance, few things are more vexing than an individual who can't work well with others when his organization needs him to become an integral part of a team, or a manager who flees from conflict while his group's performance suffers because they always take the easy way out in their decision making. In an era of team building and shared accountability, organizations need people to collaborate and manage conflict effectively, and coaching is a logical approach to use when people are less than optimally effective.

Collaboration is relatively easy to define as the art of working together effectively and productively. Conflict, however, is a bit trickier to describe. For one thing, conflict isn't necessarily negative. In fact, it's essential for productive collaborations. Conflict only becomes negative when it spins into personal vindictiveness, unproductive hostility, win-or-lose battles, and the like. So the ambiguous nature of conflict makes it problematic to define. In addition, what's the difference between conflict and disagreement, between conflict and debate? Where do you draw the line?

To avoid confusion about what we mean by conflict, let us define it. From our perspective, conflict has three components, with a corresponding coaching response attached to each.

• *Perceived mutually incompatible goals, rewards or values.* In other words, I can't get what I want if you get what you want. This is the perception. Coaching can help test this perception and suggest new ways of viewing clashes so goals aren't incompatible. As we've emphasized previously, coaches are constantly providing their clients with new ways to look at old situations. By providing them with additional information, by showing them how someone else handled a similar conflict, by giving someone the chance to share the fears and concerns that underlie the stated conflict, coaches can demonstrate that the seemingly incompatible may in fact be compatible.

• *Emotion.* Emotion puts the charge into conflict and makes it difficult to manage. Many managers tell us they're not afraid of conflict. They're just afraid that it won't be handled "constructively." People are afraid of what they or others will do or say in the grip of their emotions. In coaching sessions, people are encouraged to vent their emotions. By giving clients the chance to express why a given individual makes them so angry or how they fear conflict might harm a relationship, coaches get feelings on the table. In many business organizations, there are no forums for surfacing emotions. Displaying emotion may be viewed as inappropriate, thus feelings simmer and conflicts seem worse and more problematic than they really are. In a coaching situation, you'll find that once people talk about how they feel, they're better able to analyze conflict objectively.

• *Attempt to defeat the other person or arrive at a solution that is mutually satisfying to both parties.* People can turn a conflict into a win-lose situation — a battle to the death. Instead of searching for a mutually satisfactory solution, some people in conflict seek only to win. Coaching is an opportunity to explore win-win options, a chance to help a client see things from an "adversary's" perspective.

As a coach, you can use role-playing (having the client play his adversary) and other tools to walk a mile in someone else's shoes, or stand back and look at things from the shareholder's view and consider, What is the right thing to do? In the heat of battle, it's difficult for people to step back and see that someone else might have a legitimate issue; coaching provides a "step-back" environment. This doesn't mean that coaching's goal is compromise, which is a lose-lose proposition. Coaching is finding creative ways to give both parties what they require (see Exhibit 9.1).

There are many variations on the conflict-collaboration theme. Some who are involved in conflict might generously be described as difficult; their arrogance or cynicism prevents them from sharing information, patiently listening to another person, and so on. Others, however, have more subtle—and in some ways more challenging—developmental issues. They may seek consensus at the expense of productive debate. They may work well with certain types of people and not others. They may be victims of organizational policies that unwittingly provide negative sanctions against collaboration.

Exhibit 9.1. Conflict Components.

Component	Coaching Strategy
Perceived incompatible goals, rewards, values	"I can't get what I want if you get what you want." This may be an inaccurate perception, which the coach can help the client change.
Emotion	Let clients vent the emotional charge. Then they can deal with the issues more objectively.
Attempt to defeat the other person	Use role playing to help clients understand another perspective if conflict becomes a win-lose situation instead of a search for a mutually satisfactory solution.

Developing people into effective collaborators and conflict managers has become an organizational priority. Many times the stakes are huge: if division heads don't learn how to share resources and information and rise above personal animosities, the organization will never achieve its business strategy. Before talking about the techniques you can use to deal with these issues, let's consider what's driving companies to prioritize collaboration.

The Four Driving Forces

Commitment, passion, energy, and creativity flow from collaboration and are prized by organizations. As a coach, your job is to foster collaboration that releases these and other positive traits into the organization. Although companies seek these collaborative qualities for many reasons, the following are becoming increasingly important:

• *Showing one face to the customer.* Large companies with multiple product and service groups are attempting to maximize their cross-selling opportunities. They're eager to break down the silos that separate various plants, divisions, product groups, and other entities and coordinate marketing strategies, technologies, and human resources. When this call to coordination and cooperation is issued from on high, however, conflicts arise. Group leaders are suspicious of other groups' motives; they feel they're doing the lion's share of the work for little reward. We're coaching people at a large telecommunications company that's attempting to cross-sell long-distance, local phone service, wireless services, and telecommunications equipment. To say that the various groups don't understand the meaning of proactive cooperation is an understatement. Of course, after years of partisan politics, who could blame them? Coaching, however, shatters these boundaries by making people aware that they exist and demonstrating the harm they do, both to an individual's performance and to larger organizational goals. Using tools such as reflection and confrontation, coaching motivates people to cooperate.

- *Coordinating policies with practices.* Balancing corporatewide policies with common practices requires people to rise above their vested interests. We're working with a Fortune 50 company that's attempting to create a common technology platform. Even though marketing, manufacturing, research, and other groups all agree this makes sense, each of these groups has historically built its technology independently. When push comes to shove, each group has technology requirements it insists must be met — requirements that can't be met unless everyone is willing to cooperate. A good coach can open people's eyes to the big-picture needs and help them realize that standard practice no longer suffices. Coaching is a forum for exploring "small" versus "big" needs — clients can learn how meeting a big need can benefit them just as much, or more, as meeting a smaller need.

- *Increasing shared learning.* The potential of a learning organization is impossible to achieve unless different groups share customer information, product development practices, sales and marketing strategies, human resources, and manufacturing technologies. Tensions between various functions and other groups often impede any sort of exchange of ideas and information. Management, recognizing that knowledge is the new competitive edge, is desperate to dissipate the xenophobic attitudes that stand in the way of shared learning. As a coach, you can make a client aware of how her protectionistic mind-set works against the concept of a learning organization by confronting her with her practices, helping her analyze the reasons behind these practices, and developing an action plan to change the way she works.

- *Meeting development goals.* Well-rounded managers are in great demand and short supply. To expose people to a wide range of experiences, managers need to stop treating their direct reports like personal assets and view them as organizational assets. For managers who are focused on amassing power and control, this is a tough shift to make. If they don't make this shift, however, the company won't have much leadership bench strength and will be top-heavy with functional specialists. Therefore, learning to collaborate with direct reports rather than dictate to them (and engage in no-win battles) is essential (see Exhibit 9.2). Coaches can emphasize the need for bench strength and for well-rounded managers to their clients, demonstrating how an individual's power trip is preventing this need from being met.

Keeping an Eye Peeled for Certain Types of People

Certain types of people have a terrible time with conflict and collaboration. As a coach, a warning signal should sound in your head if one of these types is sitting across from you and you're

Exhibit 9.2. Forces Driving Collaboration.

Showing one face to the customer	Large companies often function in silos, which blocks cross-selling opportunities with customers. Encouraging collaboration maximizes the company's ability to profit as a whole.
Coordinating policies with practices	Organizational divisions often develop their own ways of doing business. Leveraging internal resources (technology, policies, and so on) creates consistency and cost-effectiveness across divisions.
Increasing shared learning	If groups don't share best practices, the organization loses opportunities to advance. Internal competition and blocks can prevent sharing learning.
Meeting development goals	When managers focus on amassing personal power, they treat employees as personal rather than organizational assets. This creates functional specialists, and leaves the organization top-heavy without general managers.

dealing with business goals that require someone to work productively with others. Here are five distinct personalities to watch
out for:

Introverts

This is a very common type when it comes to poor collaboration
and conflict management skills. Because they keep so much inside
and aren't tuned in to the outside world, they may create conflict
without even being aware of it. When they are aware of conflict,
they often avoid the confrontation necessary to resolve it; confrontation makes them uncomfortable and they don't know how to
handle the feelings it engenders. Similarly, they resist collaboration
because they don't readily share their ideas and opinions. Introverts
who play key roles in projects or are members of important strategic teams can create big problems because they may keep key ideas
or pieces of information to themselves.

Pleasers

This type is not as obviously dysfunctional when it comes to collaboration and conflict issues. On the surface, pleasers may appear
to be great team players and have no trouble at all with conflict.
Desperate to be seen as nice and cooperative, they bend over backward to acknowledge another person's point of view. Productive
collaboration, however, is not simply being agreeable. The dan-
ger from a managerial perspective is that pleasers don't trust their
judgment and experience, readily deferring to others who are
more insistent about what they want. Their end game is making sure that someone else — a boss, a direct report — gets his way.
Although they may avoid conflict, they also avoid the sometimes contentious debate that produces great ideas. One of our
clients was a leader in his organization, and he was admired for being engaging, witty, and articulate. But the pleaser could not deliver bad news. Many times, he'd sit down with a direct report and

try and explain what that person was doing wrong, but by the end of the conversation, this pleaser had said so many nice things that it was difficult for the direct report to know whether the meeting had been called to criticize or compliment him. As good as our client was at providing support in a crisis, he just couldn't make a decision that would alienate other people. He couldn't get it through his head that sometimes he had to engage in conflict to achieve goals. As a result, he consistently fell short of goals that management set for him.

Cynics

We've talked about this type of person before, and the problem here is that cynics' words and behaviors create distrust. Nothing produces conflicts and impedes collaboration faster. Typically, cynics are skeptical of other people's intentions and demonstrate this skepticism by asking for more information than is necessary or by expressing disbelief in what someone is saying or why the person is saying it. Cynics also are contrarians, taking the opposite point of view not because they believe in it but because they derive a perverse satisfaction from preventing someone else from achieving their goal. They foment conflict not because of an honest disagreement but just for the sake of argument. Trust is at the heart of teamwork or any kind of collaboration, and cynics make trust difficult if not impossible.

False Advocates

We discussed people like this earlier; their behaviors, like those of pleasers, often appear to foster collaboration. They usually avoid open conflict, nod in agreement during meetings, and generally seem to be buying into whatever decision is reached. After the meeting, however, they may bad-mouth the decision of the group or a particular individual. Or they may agree to one thing and then do something entirely different. These people cause tremendous problems because they take conflict underground.

Egotists

Their inflated sense of self-worth prevents them from admitting they're wrong or seeing the merit of another person's position. Conflict is always a win-lose proposition for them, and collaboration works only if they can convince someone else to adopt their approach. One of the qualities organizations prize in their managers and leaders is the ability to see issues from another person's perspective. Arrogant individuals have great difficulty seeing beyond their own point of view.

Sometimes the personality issues are more subtle and a measurement tool such as FIRO-B helps identify subtleties such as an individual's need for and desire to express inclusion, control, and affection. Many times, conflicts revolve around these needs.

We worked with a CEO who was on the verge of firing his recently hired COO. The CEO had been walking around the company's factories and often hearing complaints about who the COO had promoted and other decisions he had made. The COO, on the other hand, felt the CEO could not let go, was overly involved in the COO's areas of responsibility, and was second-guessing his decisions.

After administering the FIRO-B to the CEO and COO, we found that they were both high-control individuals and that this need for control (as well as the need to express it) was generating much of the conflict. In addition, the FIRO-B indicated that the CEO also had a great need for inclusion, and the COO's decisions made the CEO feel out of the loop.

Talking with both of these top executives about their needs didn't magically enable each to empathize with the other. What it did do, however, was allow them to examine their relationship from another perspective. They began to understand that it was futile to keep insisting the other had to change; it also helped them realize that their own needs were skewing their opinions of each other. They eventually detached themselves emotionally from the conflict and began examining the issues more objectively.

What the Organization Contributes to Collaborative Problems

Although these personality types certainly have problems with collaboration and conflict, many other types of people also have problems with it. It's tempting for a coach to jump to conclusions and assume that the client's personality is the cause of these problems. Perhaps it is. But you should also examine the organizational environment for root causes. Here are the most common organizational issues that cause people to short-circuit when conflict arises:

Matrix Structures

These structures wreak havoc with people's ability to handle conflict and collaboration. Such a structure sets up dual reporting responsibilities, and people end up torn between divisional and functional objectives. Although these objectives can be the same (or similar), they're often in conflict, and that produces conflicts among people. This is a big problem for team members operating under this structure. Some people on teams never gain their teammates' trust because when push comes to shove they remain loyal to their division boss. Their behaviors are similar to the personality types previously discussed, but the source of their behaviors is different. They're not pleasers, cynics, or any of the aforementioned types, but they're caught in a structure that results in the same symptomatology.

Silos

Any veteran of a culture with strong functional, geographic, or service silos immediately recognizes how these silos hamper collaboration. Sometimes the problem is simply a lack of communication and common goals; people in another function or office seem "foreign," unable to speak your language or appreciate your concerns. Other times there is outright hostility between functions. Some individuals are adept at breaking down silo-inspired tensions, whereas others are governed by the mentalities they spawn.

Policies

Some organizations say they want to foster teamwork but maintain policies or compensation practice that only reward individual performance. Sometimes one unit of a company doesn't receive credit, or perhaps even loses resources when it collaborates with another unit on a joint product offering (or any type of project); the company policy is that one unit sacrifices for the good of the organization. All sorts of policies exist that may spur individuals to resent enforced collaboration (resulting in conflict) or that provide strong incentives for me-first behaviors.

Culture

In some organizations, the anticollaboration incentives aren't as formal as written policies but they're no less effective. Cultural imperatives and taboos prevent people from working together synergistically. Perhaps the most common cultural offender in this regard involves attitudes about conflict. A conspiracy of politeness dominates these cultures—a willful suppression of debate and dissent. It's considered bad form to prevent consensus from being achieved, to challenge authority, or to take a radical position. In these cultures, conflict is swept under the rug and collaboration is in name only. It's also possible that consensus is too highly esteemed in a culture. So much emphasis is placed on having everyone on board before moving forward that conflict explodes when one or two people on a team hold on to their minority position. Not achieving consensus scares everyone to death, and a conflict arises over why these one or two people are spoiling things for the group.

Determining Whether the Issue Is Organizational

It's not always easy to determine where the problem lies. An individual may be acting cynically or displaying arrogance, suggesting that personality is the root cause. But what if the system is causing him to act this way? People's counterproductive behaviors are often because of misalignment — a disconnect somewhere in the system stops managers from collaborating effectively. To determine whether the organization your client works for is out of alignment in some way, ask the following questions:

Is there understanding and agreement on the organization's strategy, and is it connected to relevant factors in the marketplace?

Are goals and objectives for individuals and groups consistent with one another and with the overall stated direction for the business?

Are leaders on the same page with respect to what needs to be done to maximize organizational performance?

How does the organization structure support the strategy, and to what extent does it facilitate or inhibit collaboration across units?

Are the right systems in place, and do they support the business strategy?

Does the culture handle conflict effectively? Do disagreements surface and get resolved, or do they go underground?

Does the culture support the overall direction of the business?

Most coaches don't ask these types of questions, and it may be difficult for management to grant coaches this much latitude. It's also critical to examine another common area of organizational misalignment: leaders who lack the skills necessary to manage a group process. Is your client being accused of fighting with members of his team or being unable to manage conflict among his direct reports? The problem may not be your client's leadership style as much as his lack of training and experience in managing teams.

As part of your assessment, take a look (see Exhibit 9.3) at the team your client is managing and ask the following questions:

Exhibit 9.3. Addressing Organizational Issues.

Matrix structures: Dual reporting causes conflicting objectives.

Silos: Lack of cross-silo communication causes breakdowns, distancing.

Policies: Policies reward individual performance, not collaboration.

Culture: Collaboration is either not reinforced or is so highly esteemed that no one can ever disagree and false consensus gets in the way.

Questions at the Organization-Team Level

Do people understand and agree on the strategy? Is it connected to relevant factors in the marketplace?

Are individual and group goals consistent with each other and the organization strategy?

How does the organization structure support or hinder the strategy and the collaboration across business units?

Are leaders on the same page with respect to what needs to be done to maximize organizational performance?

Are the needed systems in place to support the business strategy?

Does the culture support the overall direction of the business?

How does the culture handle conflict? Do disagreements surface and get resolved, or do they go underground?

Are team members clear about their objectives and each other's roles?

Do all members have the opportunity to influence the team's work?

Do members understand their individual and team performance measures? Are these measures sufficiently challenging?

Are team members recognized for their contributions?

Do team members trust, cooperate with, and support each other?

Are conflicts resolved effectively?

The First Goal of the Coach

Conflict management can be complex and involve intertwined personality and organizational issues. It may take time to extricate the strands and get your client to see what's really happening. Therefore, it often makes sense to set a simpler initial goal: help your client develop a framework for understanding the other person's situation. This doesn't mean you have to get your client to agree with that situation or point of view; he needs to simply gain perspective. The paths to breakthroughs are paved by context. When people see situations from a broader perspective or have a fresh sense of why people do what they do, a conflict loses much of its heat.

Vic was recently brought in to a Fortune 100 company to become the head of strategic planning. As part of the deal, Vic's boss agreed that he would report directly to the CEO and wouldn't have to report to the CFO, even though the previous strategic planning head did. Barbara, the CFO, feels she has lost a turf war but doesn't openly complain about it. Instead, she tortures Vic with innuendoes and asides that prey on his insecurities. "No outsider has ever really made it here, but you let me know if I can help you in any way," she tells him. Barbara is also slow or unwilling to provide the strategic planning group with information they request and does other things that drive Vic nuts.

The conflict between Vic and Barbara simmers just beneath the surface. They don't have loud arguments or complain to other executives about each other, but they are clearly not collaborating productively. Vic wants to confront Barbara about the situation but has great difficulty doing so. For one thing, she's a woman and Vic has never been good at confronting women. For another thing, Barbara is an adroit political player and she's never really given Vic a clear target to shoot at; her obstructionism and other behaviors are adroitly manipulative, and Vic doesn't know how to approach Barbara about what she's done.

When we sat down with Vic, one of the first things we tried to do was get him to develop an alternative perspective. It's possible that Barbara was not a vindictive person determined to destroy Vic out of spite. To help him entertain this possibility, we encouraged Vic to put himself in Barbara's shoes. She is the only high-ranking woman in the corporation, we explained. She also has worked hard, creatively, and productively to achieve what she has achieved, and she's dealt with some moronic, macho men along the way. We related a story we had heard about how Barbara was torpedoed for a position early in her career by a man who felt she wasn't aggressive enough. Barbara also has received feedback that she's too quiescent and needs to fight back more.

Vic still felt that Barbara had done him wrong. But after putting her position in context, he could at least see why she felt compelled to do him wrong. One bit of progress he made was that he stopped demonizing Barbara and has since tried to engage her in more direct and honest communication. As Vic said, "I might not like her attitude, but at least I understand how the environment of this company contributed to it."

To help clients develop a broader framework and see a situation differently, explore the following questions with them:

Why do you think the other person is behaving the way he is?

Why is he dug into his position?

Is his boss or some other executive creating conditions that are causing or exacerbating your disagreement?

Do you think the two of you would have the same problems if you were working for a different type of company?

What pressure is the other person under? Do you think this pressure is contributing in any way to the conflict and how he acts toward you?

Another technique that helps clients reframe their thinking involves this question: *Why is this situation on your path of development?* This question gives managers a chance to look in the mirror and see how they are contributing to the conflict. By *path of development,* we're referring to a significant learning opportunity in the context of life's lessons. There's one type of person who always gets your goat, whose behavioral tics drive you crazy. Throughout your career, you've repeatedly become embroiled in holy wars with a certain type of person. The big-picture thinker is often hooked by the person who is obsessed with details. The highly organized individual is usually triggered by seat-of-the-pants people.

Finding the recurring pattern can help liberate a client from his conflicts by giving him a sense of who he is under certain circumstances. To get people to find these patterns, ask them:

What does this (situation, event) remind you of?

Have you ever been in this type of situation before?

Does this remind you of something that happened outside of work, especially something you remember from your childhood—when you felt you weren't trusted, lacked authority, weren't given straight answers, or were victimized by hidden agendas?

See Exhibit 9.4 for questions that address individual issues.

Tools That Can Be Incorporated into the Process

As you attempt to answer these questions and figure out what's causing your client's collaboration and conflict woes, you'll find that certain tools will support your efforts. Here are some tools we've found to be most effective, and how they can be used:

• *Interviews conducted with key people in order to understand the source of the conflict-collaboration issue and to generate a potential solution.* Focus interviews so that you can learn whether organiza-

Exhibit 9.4. Addressing Individual Issues.

Introverts: Don't share ideas and opinions; resist conflict

Pleasers: Agree or defer to avoid conflict; can't deliver bad news

Cynics: Create distrust by taking the contrary view; enjoy conflict

Passive-aggressives: Appear to agree but bad-mouth in private

Arrogants: Can't admit others are right or they're wrong; can't see others' views

Questions for the Individual

Why do you think the other person is behaving the way he or she is?

Why is the other person dug into his or her position?

Is the other person's boss creating conditions that exacerbate your disagreement?

Do you think the two of you would have the same problems if you were working for a different kind of company?

What kind of pressure is the other person under? Do you think this contributes to the conflict and how the person acts toward you?

Why is this situation on your "path of development?"

tional issues or something inside your client is causing the collaborative breaking— or whether it's a combination of both factors.

   • *Tests such as the MBTI, the CDR Leadership Risk Profile,*[1] *and the FIRO-B that you can use to determine whether your client's personal style is a major factor or whether the personalities of team or group members are a contributing cause.* If your client doesn't fit one of the personality types mentioned earlier, a test like this might be called for.

   • *Reflection that allows your client (and members of your client's group) to reflect on her actions and how they are contributing to your client's problems or development issues.* Don't just say to your client, "Now I want you to reflect on why you and Jerry can't get along."

[1] CDR Assessment Group (1998), Tulsa, Okla.

Instead, set up this request with a discussion that motivates your client to consider the issue seriously and deeply. Talk about how her boss and her boss's boss are disappointed that she hasn't seized the opportunity to work better with others; share feedback that illustrates your general conclusions that she has problems with conflict. Make your points powerfully so that reflection is something she wants to do, not something she has to do.

• *Confronting behaviors that are making collaboration difficult and asking clients to acknowledge conflicts and the role they've played in fomenting them.* Use this tool when a more subtle method fails to produce results. Some people are in deep denial when it comes to being aware of collaborative difficulties — they are adamant about how well they work with people. Confronting, if done forcefully and without rancor, can sometimes jar people into reality.

• *Observing your client as he is having trouble working with someone or when he becomes enmeshed in unproductive arguments, especially when he is working as part of or leading a team.* Your mere presence will make him more aware of his behaviors and how they affect others. You can also use your observations for more effective coaching discussions and confrontations.

• *Real-time feedback that gives your client a sense of what he is doing when he is doing it; telling a client what you've observed and how you think this contributes to the collaborative issue at hand.* In other words, don't wait for your scheduled coaching session. Pull your client off to the side and review what just took place while it's fresh.

• *Teaching clients what they might do.* Collaboration and conflict challenges often leave clients not knowing what to do, and coaching can provide clients with information and techniques that will help them take steps in the right direction (see Exhibit 9.5). Sit down and give your client an assignment for which you both hold him accountable. Have him attempt to work on a job with someone he's never worked well with; have him take the risk of disagreeing with his boss when he's convinced he's right (rather than backing off as he usually does). Rehearse the interaction and provide your client with ways that he can handle it more effectively.

Exhibit 9.5. Collaboration and Constructive Conflict Tools.

Tool	Why Used
Interviews	Conduct these with key people to help you understand the issue and identify possible solutions.
Tests	Use tests to determine the client's personality type and how that might influence the conflict and ability to collaborate.
Reflection	Use this tool so the client and individual in the conflict can seriously consider the situation and implications.
Confrontation	When necessary, confront behaviors contributing to the conflict to jar people out of the current situation.
Observation	Observe the client in a difficult situation, and discuss observations and potential improvements.
Real-time feedback	Pull the client aside during or after a conflict situation rather than wait for a scheduled coaching session.
Teaching design	Use this specific learning program to help the client develop new skills.

We used many of these tools with Jack, the chief information officer for a Fortune 500 company. The company's goal for Jack was that he leverage information technology opportunities across the business that would affect the bottom line. Jack was having a problem achieving this objective, in part because his team was awash in conflicts. This five-member team reported to different divisional heads as well as to Jack. Establishing a common technology platform for the company was something their division heads resisted; each had specific information technology needs and reflexively resisted any change. This created a great deal of acrimonious debate within the team and prevented them from moving forward. Jack needed to learn to manage conflict in order to achieve the over-arching business goal.

After meeting with Jack, we interviewed each member of his team, asking questions about the clarity of the information technology strategy, team working relationships, Jack's performance as the team leader, and so on. After analyzing the results of these interviews, we identified the areas that seemed to be causing intra-team conflicts. One area involved Jack's failure to clearly articulate the information technology strategy, coupled with team members' needs to prioritize divisional requirements. After sharing these results with both Jack and his team, they saw the source of many of the pitched battles that had hampered their progress. We also administered CDR Assessments,[1] the Myers-Briggs Type Indicator, and FIRO-B tests to everyone on the team and again shared and discussed the results. From these results, it was clear that one member of the team — an introvert — was making a bad situation worse. Although the matrix structure that governed the team certainly was causing problems and making Jack less effective than he might have been, this team member had great difficulty working with others, and this difficulty manifested itself in temper tantrums that ended long periods of frustrated silence. In addition, the results of Jack's profile indicated that he was poor at execution and tended to avoid conflict wherever possible.

Based on what we learned from interviewing and the profiles — and how Jack and the team members reacted to our feedback — we took the following steps:

- Worked with Jack to change his personal leadership style

- Interviewed various division leaders to determine what they expected of information technology and how they saw it contributing to business performance improvement

[1]CDR Assessment Group (1998), Tulsa, Okla.

- Brainstormed with Jack and his team on ways to meet the team's goals without compromising division business results

- Provided real-time feedback to Jack and team members as they worked together (confronting tool)

- Conducted a visioning session with the team, helping them to conceive what they might achieve and how they might get to that point

- Shared models for organizational change and conflict resolution that Jack was unfamiliar with (teaching tool)

As of this writing, Jack is still struggling with some of these issues, but he and his team have made real progress. At the very least, any observer of Jack and his team can see that they've made great strides in managing conflict in productive ways.

The Trick to Coaching the Conflicted

Some people avoid conflict with amazing diligence and dexterity. Others can't get enough of it. Some of the former group deny they avoid conflict, whereas some of the latter group insist conflict isn't a problem because "I'm right and the other person is wrong."

Conflict issues can bedevil coaches. The challenge isn't simply to help people stop arguing with one direct report or start learning to confront the boss. Rather, it's to help them learn how to handle all types of people in a wide variety of situations in which conflict is an issue. Temporary changes in behavior aren't sufficient. People need to experience profound changes in behaviors and attitudes if they're going to achieve larger goals.

The following techniques may help you deal with the tricky conflict issues you'll encounter as a coach:

- *Get to the source of the problem.* When you have a client who doesn't deal with conflict, you need to investigate why that is. It's not enough for someone to say, "I don't deal with conflict well." Your client needs to dig deeper and acknowledge the source. The three source-reasons for conflict avoidance are (1) an irrational fear of confrontation, (2) an inability to perceive conflict because they're not attuned to group or organizational dynamics and simply overlook what is patently obvious to others, and (3) an inability to deal with it. When people lack the experience or tools to deal with conflict effectively, they pretend it doesn't exist or simply ignore it. Explore with your client which of these reasons pertains to him.

- *Convince people of what's at stake.* Sometimes managers don't realize how their conflict-avoidance is affecting their work performance. You need to illustrate how this avoidance prevents a team from delivering results on schedule. When clients realize that this isn't a minor problem but one that prevents them from achieving what the organization needs them to achieve, the problem hits home and they are more motivated to resolve it.

- *Encourage them to take the other person's point of view.* In heated work situations, people are amazingly locked into their own points of view. They're unable to empathize with another person's issues and therefore blame the other person for the conflict. Coaches can help people take a step back and see the other person's perspective by asking them to reflect on what is going on in this other individual's life. We had a client who was angry at her boss because he failed to give her the recognition she believed she deserved and didn't include her on some important projects. After doing our research and interviewing, we asked our client to think about why her boss was acting this way. She eventually acknowledged that he was under a great deal of pressure from management because of his own performance shortcomings. We also shared with her the fact that her boss had been accused of showing favoritism toward her by other members of their team, and she acknowledged that he may well have overreacted to those accusations. These discussions helped our client depersonalize the issue and talk about them objectively with her boss; the tremendous tension between them dissipated and they once again enjoyed a productive working relationship.

• *Find out whether people are listening to each other.* People who are locked in mortal combat don't listen to each other. They're so busy trying to win an argument and convince others of the right-ness of their position that they tune out their combatant. You can facilitate your client's ability to resolve conflict if you can help him listen to what's going on underneath the argument. What is the other person really angry about? Is the other person hearing what your client is really saying?

• *Bring other people into the process if necessary.* It's amazing how easily some conflicts can be resolved when you bring in clarifying information. People misinterpret another person's words or action and get all bent out of shape. Bringing in an eyewitness to the event often helps calm things down; this eyewitness can clear up misin-terpretations faster and more credibly than anyone else. In addi-tion, you might want to bring in someone who has resources you lack to solve the conflict: an expert who can serve as an arbiter of the dispute, a source of information who can provide the facts and figures at the core of the conflict, and so on.

The Larger Implications of Conflict

One of the great sins of coaching is to deal with conflict as an indi-vidual issue. In other words, a client complains to a coach that he's afraid of conflict and always gives in rather than disagree and force-fully state his point. The coach then helps the client learn how to win arguments, wield power, and dominate others. This type of coaching might make people into more formidable adversaries, but it does little else. It may help people learn to confront or resolve conflicts in their favor, but it's all "I" stuff and no "We."

You must always ask how the individual conflict issue relates to the organization's mission and vision and to a division's or team's goal. What is the larger entity trying to accomplish, and how can a client's behavioral changes regarding conflict contribute to achieving that mission, vision, or goal?

When you speak to your client about the performance improvement or breakthrough he needs to achieve, define it not just in individual terms but by how it will affect group goals. Your client needs to understand that he's not just learning to become a better collaborator because it's an admirable trait but because he can't do the job the organization needs him to do without it.

10

Building Relationship Skills

In recent years, business has recognized the value of empathy, emotional intelligence, trust, and honesty. In an era of teams, matrix structures, and boundaryless organizations, companies need managers who can develop a new type of relationship with a wide variety of people. They require managers who can establish rapport with everyone from direct reports to associates in other countries.

In some instances, management's recognition that someone has to be coached doesn't come about because of "bad" behaviors. A boss doesn't call us in and say, "Hal needs to be coached because his direct reports are complaining about his lack of emotional intelligence." Many times, management bring us in because a person is unable to achieve performance breakthroughs, and an astute boss deduces that the person is being held back because of his mediocre relationship-building skills. In short, the impetus can be development rather than correction of problematic behaviors.

Relationships are not always an easy area to understand or identify. Let's start out by describing what this new relationship-building competency is all about.

Why They Don't Teach This Skill in Business School

In a fast-paced, interconnected, evolving organization, trust is essential. There isn't time to document every decision or to check and recheck all the data. There also isn't time for long, drawn-out discussions designed to persuade and reassure. In addition, people should not be suspicious of the boss's motives. Such suspicion makes it impossible for a boss — or anyone else — to make commitments and work at peak capacity.

To accomplish things in this environment, you need managers who establish open, trusting relationships quickly. In theory, this sounds rather simple. In practice, it requires an interconnected set of qualities that can only be developed over time. *Emotional intelligence, empathy, intuition, openness, honesty,* and *trust* are all words that describe these qualities. It might be more helpful, however, if we illustrate these qualities through examples. We'll do so within the context of the workplace.

Recent studies on innovation indicate that if you put ten people together with high intelligence quotients versus ten people with high emotional intelligence (and a wide range of cognitive intelligence), the latter group will produce more innovative ideas. This is because cognitively intelligent people don't necessarily have the ability to build on other people's ideas; they're not always able to sense someone else's frustration and back off. Emotionally intelligent people, however, are much better suited to collaborative efforts. They stimulate each other's creativity, pool capabilities, and harvest the group's best ideas. To achieve the goals of many organizations—building strong internal teams, forging alliances with outside organizations, partnering with vendors—emotional intelligence is often more valuable than individual brilliance. In fact, individually brilliant people are sometimes the ones who have the most difficulty forming synergistic relationships.

The problem isn't always that an individual is awful at building relationships but that she isn't using this skill to maximum capacity. One of our clients is a merger-and-acquisitions professional who is constantly negotiating with foreign investors, representatives from takeover targets, and her own management. Although she's skilled at building relationships with some of these people, she's not as adept with others. Her empathy is limited to certain individuals in certain situations. For instance, empathy escapes her when she attempts to persuade management to do a deal they're reluctant to make. She is unable to read the situation when management doesn't back her up and deal, and she responds angrily, alienating those in a position to help her the next time. Our coaching goal is to help her become more consistent in her relationship building and not just use this skill on occasion.

In fact, many of our clients have good emotional intelligence scores. The problem is that their emotional intelligence flickers on and off, as if there's a faulty connection. Typically, people are great at developing solid relationships with people who are just like they are—people with the same educational background, work function, social interests, and so on. They're able to know what another person is feeling because if they were in that situation, that's how they would probably feel. In a diverse workplace, however, it's essential to relate to people who are different.

This is difficult for many managers to do because of their tendency to stereotype. Rather than deal with the individual personality, we view someone through the lens of a group: "He's a classic Generation X guy" or "She's got that marketing mentality." When we stereotype, we don't react to the data before our eyes. Thus we are unable to empathize. We may think we understand another person and are empathizing, but what we are really doing is empathizing with a fiction—one that may contain some reality but not enough to matter. Astute coaching helps people transcend stereotypes and really understand the hopes, fears, needs, and visions of the individual; it enables them to stop seeing people in terms of stereotypical categories such as "customers" or "bosses" and start thinking about them as unique people. Trusting, open relationships form only when a manager "gets" who another person is. When a manager grasps what's driving—and scaring—a person, that person will naturally communicate better with the manager.

The real coaching breakthrough for many clients is reaching the point where they get it. *Getting it* means understanding other people's hopes and dreams as well as their anxieties. Getting it isn't always a cognitive process; it's often intuitive, almost a sixth sense about who another person really is. People who get it have their phone calls returned promptly; they generate passion and commitment; their people are willing to work harder and longer; they can build relationships that operate on an emotional shorthand, saving precious time in the quest to meet deadlines.

The Traits of Tremendous Relationship Builders

Certain traits define the best relationship builders in organizations, and you're likely to be coaching people who need to develop these qualities. *Empathy* and *emotional intelligence* are two good umbrella terms for these traits, but let's try and be more specific about what they entail. Organizations place a premium on the following relationship-building characteristics:

Intuition

Known as a hunch or a gut instinct, this trait has become increasingly important at a time when all the data can't be gathered before a decision is made. Making decisions with imprecise data is a given in time-sensitive, rapidly changing environments. Sensing when someone is the right person to hire and having a feeling that you can work productively with a new vendor are important attributes in relationship building. Is the person proposing a deal being completely honest? Is a customer saying one thing but implying something else? We no longer have the luxury of doing exhaustive research; we need to trust our intuition.

Two-Way Communication

Dynamic listening is just as important as conveying information clearly and convincingly. We coach a lot of people who are inarticulate and a lot who are figuratively deaf. Although these flaws may not have harmed command-and-control relationships, they harm today's relationships. The ability to deliver a compassionate but clear performance appraisal or to cultivate and understand feedback cannot be underestimated. The latter attribute is especially important. When people feel they've been heard and understood, they feel a sense of commitment to the other person (especially if that person is their boss).

Ability to Create Emotional Energy

This trait involves turning people on, getting them excited, motivated, and inspired to achieve a goal. Managers who are adept at creating this energy don't simply give rah-rah speeches or provide monetary incentives (or negative sanctions if people fail). Instead, they manufacture this energy by igniting feelings in others. Is someone feeling concerned about his career? Then the relationship-building manager demonstrates how the successful completion of an assignment can be a career-enhancing move. By seizing on a concern, fear, goal, or need, the manager creates tremendous energy. We're coaching a CEO who has just initiated his fifth workforce reduction in less than two years. It's not enough for him to explain his decision in terms of costs, market share, operating expenses, or demands from the board of directors. If he doesn't feel what his people are feeling—survivor's guilt, anxiety, uncertainty, depression—then he won't be able to muster the energy necessary for the healing process. Although we can tell him what people are going through, he has to get it and then show that he gets it. If he isn't on the same emotional wavelength as his people, nothing he does will cause them to be energized and committed to moving forward.

Clients Who Lose Control

A significant number of our coaching clients experience difficulty because they are out of touch with their own feelings and therefore don't recognize how these feelings lead to unproductive behaviors. This makes it difficult for them to adjust their behaviors to different people. They have a uniform response that doesn't take into account the personality or position of the person they're dealing with. Our goal is to help them learn to develop a range of responses based on their feelings and to be able to express them fully at times and to control them at other times.

People who don't have control of their responses may be successful individually. Just about every large company has at least one person in a position of power who routinely explodes. He maintains his power because of a significant talent—he gets deals done or is great at bringing in business—but he also saps energy from the company with his explosive feelings. Many times, others defer to him not because they agree with his position but because they know the titanic struggle that will ensue if they disagree. For the most part, these out-of-control individuals have relationships in name only; they don't motivate or inspire anyone.

Here are two examples that illustrate why organizations are so concerned about top executives who can't control their responses effectively. We were asked to call the managing director of a large foreign company by one of his top executives. While we were talking on the phone, he misunderstood who we were; he thought we were employees in his company's domestic division. His tone was combative and accusatory. "Why are you bothering me with this?" was the question he communicated. When we made clear who we were, his tone changed. Suddenly he was charming and accommodating. It was clear that this managing director had a specific style he used with subordinates—a style that reflected his impatience. Although he could display different responses to this feeling with outsiders, he didn't feel compelled to do so with insiders.

We also coached a CEO of a large technology company who lost his temper when he became frustrated. Luckily, he recognized the damage his temper caused and hired a COO. The COO was a prominent professional in the industry and greatly facilitated the turnaround the CEO was leading. Their partnership was effective, and the CEO created the vision and mapped the strategy while the COO executed it internally and handled the people problems expertly. During this partnership, profits rose in tandem with the stock price. Everyone was happy until the CEO lost it one day. During a meeting, the CEO turned on his COO and was emotionally abusive. That was it for the COO. A trusting, sensitive man, he lost all the respect he had for the chief executive and found it impossible to trust him as he once had. Less than two months after this incident, the COO departed and the company's fortunes suffered. One outburst and one broken relationship was all it took to wound this large corporation.

Where to Start

To help someone who has difficulty forming relationships may seem like a daunting task. Even for an experienced coach, it's a challenge to figure out how to help someone develop missing relationship skills. As you can see from what we've discussed so far, there are many issues involved, and counterproductive behaviors are often deeply ingrained; the development learning curve can also be steep. It may even seem presumptuous to think that anyone can turn a manager who doesn't have a clue about what his people are thinking into an empathetic, intuitive individual.

Well, perhaps that type of transformation is difficult but it is not impossible, and it certainly is possible to achieve significant performance breakthroughs in the relationship area. The key is to use a systematic approach. Rather than delve into the past (childhood memories of a cold, unresponsive parent, for instance) for answers or taking a vague, unstructured approach (talking about feelings about other people), our preferred methodology is to gather information in a goal-directed manner. The following steps will guide your efforts:

- *Discover the pattern or relationship theme; figure out what your client is doing and how others are reacting to him.* You may have been told what a client's relationship problem is and how this is preventing him from achieving certain goals by the person who brought you in to coach. But don't take one person's word for it. Talk to direct reports, supervisors, and peers to ascertain what the real relationship issue is. Are they all saying your client never listens? Do they all insist that she fails to involve the entire team? It may be that your organization already has certain feedback devices in place that will provide you with some of this information.

- *Establish why there is a need for someone to change.* In other words, why is improving relationships important to a given individual? People need to know how this change will help them in their careers and how it will enable the organization to achieve its objectives. Spelling out the connection through the data you collect is crucial. Without that, your client won't be motivated to change. He needs to understand what's in it for him and for the organization. Once he realizes that establishing better relationships will lead to more sales and that the company believes its long-term growth is tied to salespeople partnering with customers rather than just selling to them, he has two compelling reasons to change.

- *Help people understand their feelings.* This sounds obvious, but it's astonishing how many managers are out of touch with how they feel at work. Too often, they just react without thinking or reflecting about the emotions directing their words and deeds. The result is everything from passive-aggressive behavior to denial, and relationships suffer. Sensitizing people to their emotions is a good tactic. Talk to a client about a typical situation at work and see if he mentions any relationship issues. For instance, let's say he responds, "I don't know why, but Joe always bothers me." Suggest that your client intensify his self-observation the next time he meets with Joe. Ask him to pay attention to his own physical reactions. Does his pulse quicken? Does he start to tap his foot? Is there a tight feeling in the pit of his stomach? What thoughts are going through his head when he talks with Joe? What tone of voice does he use?

Keeping a journal is another way to sensitize people to their feelings. This may not work with everyone—some managers are uncomfortable putting their emotions down on paper—but it can provide a good perspective on what those feelings are and how they affect relationships over time.

- *Contrast an individual's intentions with his behaviors.* This is especially useful when a client's thinking is muddled about what she wants to accomplish in a relationship. Clarifying intention and behavior and the gap between the two can illuminate a relationship-building flaw. For instance, a client we're working with sincerely wants to be more supportive of his direct reports. This intention, however, is thwarted by his behavior of challenging his direct reports and even belittling their work. In an illogical way, this person really believes that challenge and harsh criticism is a way of demonstrating his support; he wouldn't criticize them if he didn't care about them. It is only when we showed him the gap between his intention and behaviors—when we demonstrated that he had the right idea but the wrong execution—that he got it.

- *Determine relationship expectations.* This is a good diagnostic tool for spotting the cause of a relationship breakdown. What typically happens is that relationships are stable for weeks, months, or even years because both people are meeting the other's expectations. Then one person changes. In work situations, changes may happen because one person attended a training program and learned assertiveness skills or was inspired by a guru's talk suggesting that people need to be more confrontational to be effective. For whatever reason, one individual in the relationship changes and the other one doesn't. Suddenly, expectations are out of whack. One person's role in the relationship may have been as a good listener, and now that person is stating opinions more and listening less. This creates friction in the relationship. Although some people are able to renegotiate their expectations and accommodate them, many end up fighting and feuding. Or one individual attempts to

get the other to return to old behaviors in order to get old expectations met. Exploring what these expectations are and how and why
they might have changed over time can help your client discover
the source of a relationship problem.

• *Identify relationship boundaries.* Most relationships have
boundaries but they're not always articulated. What are the taboos
in your client's relationship with his boss? Is the boss's disturbing tendency to promise great rewards but never deliver on them off limits?
Is the direct report never allowed to question his boss's decisions?
Talking about these boundaries and whether they've been violated
gives clients a fresh perspective on where a relationship went wrong.
Once they're aware of the boundaries and who violated them, they
have a path they can pursue to repair the damage or decide, with
the other person, whether the boundaries should be changed.

• *Compare and contrast perceptions.* How do you see your direct
report, and how does she see you? How do you see yourself, and how
does your direct report see herself? These simple questions can yield
a goldmine of information for clients. Again, the gaps can be huge.
We've had people tell us they perceive themselves as easygoing and
open and hear their direct report describe them as impatient and
close-minded. There's nothing like the shock of contrasting perceptions to get a client focused on relationship issues.

Tools to Turn Relationships Around

We use a variety of tools to help people do everything from deal
with difficult people to transform their entire approach to relationships. Here are the tools we use most frequently and some tips about
how to use them:

The RDA Approach

The letters stand for resent-demand-appreciate, and it's a way for
coaches to help their clients uncover feelings about problematic relationships. Too often, people keep these feelings to themselves or

aren't even aware of what their true feelings are. Articulating them can create the self-awareness necessary to change the way they approach these relationships. The RDA process requires the coach to help their clients do the following:

- *Identify what the other person is doing that he resents, dislikes, and wants stopped.* An example is, "I resent it when you sell more work than we can possibly deliver on, and you don't communicate our limits to the customer." You can role-play this dialogue with your client or you can have him write it. The point isn't to have him confront the person with whom he has a problematic relationship as much as it is to surface the feelings underlying the problem. The word *resent* need not be used. It is a device to help the client comprehend his own strong feelings.

- *Issue a "demand" for what he wants the other person to stop doing.* Again, the point isn't to issue the actual demand as much as to formulate it and get it into consciousness: "I demand that you check with our department before making a commitment to the customer and see what delivery schedule is realistic." Some people are surprised to see what they really want out of the other person in the relationship.

- *Express appreciation for the other person.* The goal here is to try and uncover the reasons someone is doing what she is doing. In other words, the objective is to create empathy for another's actions. As a coach, you want to encourage your client to put himself in the other person's shoes and get a sense of the issues that affect her decisions: "I appreciate that you have a difficult sales quota to fill and that you're under enormous pressure."

After Action Review

This is an army tool used to analyze battlefield decisions and actions. The idea is that if you look back at what went wrong or could have been improved on, you'll be able to do better the next time. From an Action Coaching standpoint, you simply need to look back at a client's interactions with a given individual and ask what went wrong and what could have been improved on. Ask your client to describe what he said and did in a recent encounter, and then dissect what went wrong.

How to Assess Assumptions

People labor under explicit and implicit assumptions that can have a negative impact on relationships. For instance, here are some common explicit assumptions: "Those guys in finance can't be trusted" or "People in senior management give lip service to delegating decisions downward but they don't really mean it." As a coach, you need to identify, challenge, and change these assumptions. We've found that many people who have problems with relationships are operating under faulty assumptions. We encourage clients to move away from assumptions that are beyond their control—"Jack just doesn't like me"—to assumptions that are consistent with their goals—"If I make a good case for my proposal, I have a chance of gaining Jack's approval."

Implicit assumptions are more difficult for coaches to identify, let alone challenge and change. Because they lurk below the surface, they require a certain amount of questioning to bring into the open. For instance, let's say someone's implicit assumption is that bosses always get their way. Here are some questions you might ask that would identify this assumption:

COACH: It seems like you refuse to challenge your boss; why is that?
EMPLOYEE: Because he'll get angry and upset if I do.
COACH: What will happen if he gets angry and upset?
EMPLOYEE: I'll just give in.
COACH: Why would you do that?
EMPLOYEE: Because he's bound to win anyway.

Normally, of course, it would take more questions than this to arrive at the implicit assumption. The point, however, is that coaches need to help their clients search for them by asking questions.

• *Examine actions that follow assumptions.* In other words, don't limit your analysis to the assumptions themselves. Looking at the behaviors that flow from assumptions—and working on ways to change those behaviors—is something that can have a positive impact on relationships. We're working with a senior executive whose assumption in difficult situations is, "If we don't do something fast, we'll never get it done." As a result of this assumption, she uses strong-arm tactics to reach agreement. Although she usually comes across as bright and friendly, deadlines bring out her anxiety and she steamrolls people to achieve consensus on a decision. Naturally, this plays havoc with her relationships. As we worked with her, we identified her assumption and the resulting behaviors, coming up with alternative actions when she's tempted to follow her old assumption. Asking, "Are we all in agreement?," allowing disagreement to occur, revisiting old decisions to make sure that no one has another point of view, taking a deep breath, and reflecting on whether her anxiety in response to deadlines is rational—these and other alternatives have allowed her to change both her assumption and her behaviors. See Exhibit 10.1 for a summary of the procedure for turning relationships around.

The Coach's Job: Aiming for More Than Nice Relationships

Terms such as *empathy* and *emotional intelligence* might make many of you nervous. As you've read about the need to help people understand their feelings, you may have wondered about some of this touchy-feely advice. We want to be clear that the job of a coach is not to help people become empathetic because that will make them more pleasant or more humanistic individuals. Emotional

Exhibit 10.1. Turning Relationships Around.

Helping People Build Relationships		Tools to Turn Relationships Around
Discover the pattern or relationship theme.	**The RDA Approach** ⇨	Have the client identify what needs to change, request a change, and express appreciation for the other person
Establish why the client needs to change.	**After Action Review** ⇨	Review past actions to determine what can improve.
Help the client understand his or her feelings.	**Assess Assumptions** ⇨	Help the client identify assumptions and change to ones that are more useful and functional.
Contrast the individual's intentions with his or her behaviors.	**Examine Actions That Follow Assumptions** ⇨	Adjust actions and behaviors to reflect more useful and functional assumptions.
Determine relationship expectations.		
Identify relationship boundaries.		
Compare and contrast perceptions.		

sensitivity to oneself and others is crucial for managing relationships in order to achieve specific organizational goals.

For instance, let's say you're coaching a high-achiever who rarely if ever praises others and frequently criticizes them. As a result, this manager is unable to keep people for long, and those he does keep are often unmotivated—no matter what they do, they never even receive a pat on the back (and often receive a figurative slap across the face) and lack any inclination to try harder or take risks. This manager's team, however, has a pivotal role in a new change initiative. It they're unable to meet the ambitious objectives that management has set for them, the entire initiative could be compromised.

Helping your client develop into a more sensitive person who shares his feelings compassionately and articulately becomes an organizational goal. As you work with your client you discover that he's tremendously hard on himself. Even though this feeling may be self-motivating, it also spills over into his behavior toward others—he's as hard on them as he is on himself. You learn that he doesn't praise others because he knows he's done a good job and assumes others also know and therefore don't need to be told. Why in the world do others have to be told they've done well, he wonders? Making this manager aware of this self-talk and the negative consequences can be a good first step toward helping him change what he says to himself. This is the fastest and most effective route to motivate the manager to praise more and criticize less. It will lead him to the behaviors required for the team's work on the change initiative.

Managers need to examine how they treat themselves and verbalize an objective self-assessment. Again, this may seem irrelevant to accomplishing business goals, but there's a clear correlation. Vince, for instance, was a tremendously self-critical executive who was being asked to downsize his division—a downsizing that was absolutely necessary for the company's economic well-being. Vince, however, just couldn't make himself do it. He stalled to the point of his own peril, and Vince's boss was ready to do the downsizing himself, even though he lacked Vince's firsthand knowledge of the value of each member of the division.

Vince agonized about how he had strong relationships with the people he knew he should let go and about how he couldn't bear to fire them. We used a technique that you might find effective when coaching people who need to do an objective self-assessment. We suggested that he ask five other people—his wife, a peer, his supervisor, and so on—how they would view his downsizing if he went through with it. What would they think of his motivation, the manner in which he would do it, his purpose in carrying out this difficult task. To a person, they told Vince that he was highly skilled at breaking bad news gently, that he would communicate why he was letting each person go in a way that would enable employees to see the larger purpose, that he would bend over backward to help people find other jobs. As one person said to Vince, "If anyone has to get rid of these people, better you than anyone else." When Vince came to terms with his own feelings—how sensitive he was to hurting anyone in any way—he was finally able to carry out his assignment, and he carried it out with honesty and compassion.

It's important to point out that relationships have changed in the new business paradigm. In the old paradigm, people at different levels related like officers and enlisted men, and the "presentation" style reigned supreme. Today, relationships are much more open and much less regimented; interaction rather than presentation is the dominant mode of communication. Given all this, managers need to change their relationship styles if they're going to motivate people to work more productively and innovatively.

Many people, unfortunately, fall back on old relationship styles when they're stressed or upset. Marge, for instance, was furious that one of her direct reports never arrived anywhere on time (though she performed very well when she finally did arrive). Marge's impulse was to let her direct report have it right between the eyes; that was her reaction when we talked about it during a coaching session. What we helped her see is that the problem was more hers than her direct report's. Marge's strong feelings were out of all proportion to the offense. In the old business paradigm, however, it would have been perfectly acceptable from a business standpoint to attack her direct report. In the new paradigm, Marge's fury would have had a negative impact. Her direct report would have rebelled or started looking for another job, and her expertise would have been lost or diminished.

Marge had to learn how to own her issues rather than project them on others. Once she began to see that her anger had much more to do with who she was (someone who overreacts to bad manners or rudeness in any form) rather than her direct report's tardiness, she was able to deal with her direct report more effectively; she realized that she needed to curb her anger to deliver her message effectively.

Whatever goal an organization has for an individual, it's highly unlikely that he can achieve it on his own. Organizations have changed to the point that individuals, no matter how talented and powerful, must depend on other people to accomplish tasks. Like it or not (and many old-line managers dislike it), skills such as dynamic listening, reading body language, and reframing issues are what make or break relationships. Coaching is uniquely able to foster these skills, encouraging managers to drop their stoic poses and get in touch with their own feelings and the feelings of others.

11

Developing Customer Consciousness

M uch about the customer has changed, as evidenced by the following relatively new phrases and requirements: *rising customer service standards, voice of the customer, partnering with customers, information exchanges with customers via the Internet, anticipating rather than meeting customer needs.* The list of ways in which supplier-customer relationships have changed goes on and on. It's not just that the service bar has been raised and the competition has become more intense but that the whole nature of the customer-supplier relationship has been dramatically altered. Consider these factors:

• *The line between the customer and the supplier is blurring.* Companies such as Boeing, Apple, and other large technology companies routinely integrate the voice of the customer and customer expectations into product development.

• *Information flows freely to the customer and between customers.* In the past, organizations believed that the less the customer knew about their practices and policies, the better. Today, organizations set up Internet sites and other forums that allow customers unprecedented access to data. Companies like Johnson & Johnson and Merck also encourage their customers to communicate with each other, something that was discouraged in the past.

• *Customers expect suppliers to know more than they (customers) do.* This is quite a challenge for suppliers, who are no longer expected just to move in step with their customers up the learning curve. At Arthur Andersen, partners are judged by clients based on how well they provide new information and ideas relative to the customer's industry and competitors.

• *Everyone needs to be aware of and responsive to the customer voice.* It's not just the sales and marketing people who have to integrate the customer into their thinking. To come up with solutions to customer problems, cross-functional brainstorming is required; people in finance, MIS, and operations have to be aware of who their customers are and what their needs are. Leaders are presented with the paradox of balancing their own business goals with customer needs—it's paradoxical because sometimes these goals and needs seem to be in conflict.

• *Expansion of the definition of "customer" from external to internal.* Too often, people treat other teams and other functional co-workers as second-class citizens; they aren't overly concerned about meeting deadlines for internal people or coming up with great ideas. The result is second-class work. The concept of an internal customer mandates working as hard and as creatively for the person down the hall as the external customer a thousand miles away.

These and other factors have created all sorts of situations that require coaching interventions. Management wants its people to respond quickly and effectively to these issues, and they're finding that certain individuals aren't able or willing to change their customer consciousness. Interestingly, we're not just coaching salespeople who are encountering problems with their customers. Quite frequently, our clients include top executives as well as managers from just about every function who just don't get what their responsibility to the customer is. In some instances, we're called in because a customer has complained or expressed a concern about someone. Other times, the company has a specific customer development goal for a given individual. In all cases, there are certain customer behaviors and attitudes that organizations want to foster. Let's look at the most common ones.

Five Consciousness-Raising Requirements

Management wants its people to become more sensitive to and connected with their customers. Here are five specific coaching guidelines for increasing this sensitivity and connectedness:

1. *Demonstrate passion and enthusiasm for customer goals.* Although most people are positive and forceful in their customer relationships, they lack the higher level of commitment and energy that is quickly becoming the standard. Instead of waiting to be told what to do or carrying out orders efficiently but dispassionately, the requirement is for initiative, anticipation, and fervor.

2. *Develop a trusting customer relationship.* Customers sense a lack of connection with certain people. They're perfectly polite and efficient, but they aren't completely open and responsive. This is a holdover from an era in which salespeople believed that the "customer is out to get you." Skepticism about a customer's motives still marks many relationships. For customers to trust suppliers, suppliers have to trust customers first.

3. *Create a sense of customer mission and purpose.* We're working with an executive who is brilliant at motivating his people to go the extra mile for the customer. They think nothing of spending a weekend brainstorming ideas for customers or researching issues that previously would have been far outside the supplier area of responsibility. This executive has elevated the customer in the minds of his direct reports, and they in turn are zealous in their efforts on behalf of the customer.

4. *Understand a customer's larger business issues.* In other words, people have to jettison the old seller mentality. If they're only concerned about the specific things they sell rather than providing value through service, information, and ideas, they won't sustain

the relationship. Customers are looking for suppliers who have insights about where their industries are heading and can offer original thinking about how to capitalize on these trends.

5. *Learn how to read the customer organization*. Managers need to pick up clues and signals indicating what customers want, not just respond to what customers say. This can involve building solid friendships with members of the customer's organization so that you're aware of shifts in power and responsibility early on. It might mean that managers have to do political mapping—determining how key people feel about an initiative that affects their company or figuring out the marketing, financial, and other concerns that are pushing them in certain directions.

In most coaching relationships, however, these general requirements translate into very specific needs, both for the individual being coached and the sponsoring organizations. Let's look at some examples of people in need of coaching and how the process can create dramatic performance improvement, breakthrough, and transformation.

Three Cases of Customer Relationships in Crisis

We work with a major consulting firm that has built its business on the ability to meet (and many times exceed) client expectations. It's difficult to imagine a more client-focused firm. When we're coaching partners of this firm, the number one organizational imperative is to help people who have fallen short of client expectations in some way.

Rick's Case: Working with a Difficult CFO

Rick had a troubled relationship with the CFO of the firm's biggest client. In fact, the CFO has threatened to pull her company's business and look elsewhere if Rick doesn't improve the quality of service. At first, Rick told us that the CFO was being unreasonable and that it was impossible to meet her notion of high-quality service because perfection isn't a realizable goal. Although there was some truth in what Rick was saying—this CFO was known throughout her own company as a perfectionist—the fact of the matter was that the CFO's dissatisfaction had to be dealt with, and Rick was the person who had to deal with it.

We encouraged Rick to move past his defensiveness and anger and explore whether there were any legitimate sources of service dissatisfaction the CFO might have. After some discussion, he admitted that he didn't visit the company very often, but he had stayed away because of his dislike for the CFO and his belief that the feeling was mutual. After looking at some additional feedback, we drew the conclusion that the CFO may well have been unhappy with Rick because he stayed away from their offices as much as possible. Our coaching, however, wasn't designed simply to foster greater self-awareness on Rick's part but to produce a significant performance improvement. To that end, we strategized with Rick about what he might do to meet this CFO's expectations. Visiting more often was an obvious answer, but it still seemed insufficient. Ultimately, we hit on the idea of Rick asking for an office at the client's headquarters that he could work out of at least once a week. The client was glad to give Rick an office, and in the next six months his relationship with the CFO improved tremendously. She appreciated the commitment he was making by spending one day a week in their offices. Even more important, Rick got to know the CFO better, and their increased interaction helped them establish a more trusting relationship, which ultimately led to more business for the firm.

Sam's Case: Failing to Connect with Internal Customers

Sam is in charge of information technology for a midsized company. His internal customers are the line people his products and services support. Sam's problem is that his customers aren't always buying what he's selling. In many cases, they've been sticking with old systems that were in place before Sam joined the company or they're purchasing systems from outside vendors. The organization has great faith in Sam's expertise but knows he's not connecting with many of his internal customers. For the company to reap the maximum benefits of this expertise, they need Sam to stop taking the line people for granted and begin treating them like customers.

As we coached Sam, we learned that his high level of expertise had fostered a certain arrogance. He felt that if the line people didn't recognize or deserve the quality of product and service he was giving them. At the smaller company he used to work for, he was considered a guru and his systems were automatically used; his advice was unquestioningly accepted. During our time together, we showed Sam some feedback from people in the organization, and he was shocked at the misunderstanding and misconceptions that were rampant about some of the software he had designed. He was also upset that some people in the company thought that management had overestimated his skills. During the coaching process, we determined that Sam was not completely to blame for this situation. The organization had pretty much thrown Sam to the wolves; the company had a tradition of allowing each department to buy its own software and contract with outside vendors to meet their needs. Sam was the first information technology director who was given the mandate to change this tradition. Unfortunately, he wasn't given much support in this endeavor.

Part of the solution, therefore, was for the organization to communicate Sam's role and its desire to bring its information technology products and services completely in-house. It also involved setting up a system of internal contracting procedures where funding for projects was contingent on meeting internal customer requirements. Sam became much more accountable for both providing the right types of products and explaining how they worked to the line people they were designed for. Over time, Sam became adept at recognizing who his customers were and what they needed; he also became skilled at shaping the internal customers' expectations about what would be delivered and how long it would take to deliver it.

Janice's Case: Treating Customers and Staff Differently

Janice was a sales manager with a large Fortune 500 company, and we had been called in to work with her because some of her customers had been complaining about her group's slow response time as well as other issues. When we began meeting with Janice and shadowed her to observe her interactions with customers, we expected to find some obvious shortcoming. In fact, we'd never seen anyone as skillful in communicating with customers. She asked the right questions, listened carefully, exercised patience, established trust, and avoided defensiveness when the customer expressed dissatisfaction. She also seemed to return calls and send requested information promptly. For a while, we were stumped as to what we might recommend or how we might help Janice. Then we observed her with her staff. In response to a customer complaint, she called them in for a meeting and exploded. It was as if we were watching Janice's evil twin sister. All her patience was gone. In its place was nastiness and invective. It soon became clear that Janice's approach with her staff was demoralizing and was preventing them from providing the customer service of which they were certainly capable.

This situation isn't all that unusual. Some managers are so obsessed and meticulous about providing superior customer service that they focus their energy on this one task, and they may well establish great one-on-one customer relationships. But if they manhandle their own people, they sabotage themselves. Time and again, we've found that customer satisfaction is tied to employee satisfaction. If direct reports feel their needs are being met, they're much more likely to meet the needs of customers.

It took a number of conversations, different sources of feedback and benchmarking this type of situation in another company before Janice achieved her performance breakthrough. Eventually, she realized the indirect damage she was doing to her customer by ranting and raving at her direct reports. She gradually repaired that damage by being highly conscious of her tendency to blame and berate employees when something went wrong with a customer.

Techniques and Tools for Building Customer Relationships

Although our coaching process applies to customer issues, we keep the steps shown in Exhibit 11.1 in mind as we move through the process.

These steps keep us and our client focused on an organizational standard for working with customers. For example, we work with one company that has created a formal list of expectations for customer service. One of the managers we're coaching has not met some of the expectations on the list and consequently is having problems with one of her customers. Though she's doing well in many areas, she's come up short in the area of innovative thinking; she wasn't meeting the customer expectation of out-of-the-box thinking. Customer interviews reaffirmed that she wasn't meeting this particular expectation and the feedback we gave her was very

Exhibit 11.1. Improving Customer Relations.

Raising Customer Consciousness

Demonstrate passion and enthusiasm for customer goals.

Develop a trusting customer relationship.

Create a sense of customer mission and purpose.

Understand a customer's larger business issues.

Learn how to read the customer organization.

Tools for Raising Customer Consciousness

Set specific expectations as to what excellent customer service looks like.

Provide feedback to the person about how well (or poorly) the person is meeting these expectations.

Develop a plan to close the gap between expectations and current performance.

explicit in this regard, including direct quotes from the customer. But because the expectation was crystal clear, we could create a very specific plan to deal with it. We delineated the customer areas where creative solutions were especially important and suggested some creativity exercises and approaches to use when problems came up in these areas.

Sometimes, of course, organizations aren't clear about their customer service expectations. They may recognize that a particular manager is having problems with a customer and that he doesn't establish the same bond of trust and understanding as other managers, but they're vague about what the customer really wants. All the organization knows is that the manager better improve his customer service or they may lose a customer.

In these situations coaches must probe with the manager, his supervisor, and sometimes customers themselves to determine expectations. To get started, ask your client and his boss the questions shown in Exhibit 11.2.

Next, gather whatever written material is available—job descriptions, performance objectives, and so on—that provide additional insight about these expectations and whether they are being met. Perhaps the most useful step—and sometimes the most problematic—is to interview your client's customers and obtain their feedback. Adapting the questions listed earlier and asking them directly of customers usually yields crucial information about

Exhibit 11.2. Customer Consciousness Questions.

Customer Consciousness Questions for the Client

What do your customers want?

What would success look like if your customers were really satisfied?

What are the challenges your customers are facing?

What are your customers' greatest needs?

How do you think you are performing against your customers' expectations?

performance strengths and weaknesses that can be filtered into a development plan.

The problematic aspect of all this, of course, is that many managers are reluctant to have any "outsider" talk to their customers. Sometimes this reluctance is pure defensiveness and needless paranoia. Other times, however, it's justified. The process of seeking feedback from customers may create new customer expectations. If, for instance, you ask a customer how well a manager understands his business, this may start the customer thinking about whether this manager really does understand his business; it may cause the customer to expect this manager to spend more time at the customer's office, ask more questions, do more research, and so on. Coaches need to talk to their clients about this issue and arrive at the most effective approach. We've found that data-gathering compromises can be made so that an individual's relationship with his customer is preserved. In some instances, we've worked with our clients to develop questions we need their customers to answer, but we've had our clients ask the questions in both formal and informal ways. This keeps us out of the customer's hair and allows clients to determine the best way to keep expectations realistic.

Two Common Performance Breakthrough Goals

Increasingly, organizations are looking for customer performance breakthroughs in the following two areas: (1) they want managers to go beyond providing technical expertise and become a valued business adviser to their customers, and (2) they want managers to be aware of the impact their personal style is having on customers and change that style when appropriate.

The first goal is related to the broadening role of suppliers of all types. Organizations are recognizing that their people can no longer simply provide nuts-and-bolts information and ideas to their customers — that this is the lowest customer service expectation on the totem pole. A performance breakthrough now consists of establishing a bond of trust and communication with the customer that transcends the old transactional relationship. When customers begin bouncing their ideas off suppliers first and sharing their fears and hopes for the business with them, then the relationship has moved to the level organizations desire.

We've worked with the partners of a law firm on this goal. As technically brilliant as many of their lawyers are, they are limited in their ability to advise clients on issues that go beyond the scope of their legal expertise. One of the firm's patent attorneys, for instance, was dumbfounded when one of his clients complained that he wasn't "adding value." He immediately cited how he had helped them protect their intellectual property in all sorts of ways, but he was missing the point. His client and the management of his law firm hoped that he might offer insights about the significance of his advice, that he might suggest alternatives to his advice and how each one might play out long term for their business. It became obvious that this attorney was very quick to offer solutions and very slow to realize the ramifications of these solutions. His insistence that a patent had been violated by a competitor and that his client should sue didn't take into account that the client was partnering with this competitor on another project and a lawsuit might jeopardize a valuable relationship.

As a result of this feedback, the patent attorney began working on slowing down his knee-jerk technical reactions to problems. Rather than rely solely on his knowledge of patent law, he made an effort to listen to the worries behind a client's request for solutions and address them in his recommendations. He also worked harder at understanding the business issues confronting his clients. By slowing down, broadening his knowledge base, and relying less on his technical expertise, this attorney made the breakthrough his firm wanted him to make.

The other goal—being aware of and changing one's personal style—is especially important in an era of diversity. Understanding the impact we have on people who are different from us in some way is at the heart of this goal. It may be that we relate well to white male customers over fifty who are steeped in traditional organizational cultures but rub others the wrong way. Breakthroughs are facilitated by putting a name on the personality types involved. We use the Myers-Briggs Type Indicator (MBTI), CDR Assessment tools,[1] and FIRO-B to give our clients a sense of their personality types versus those of customers.

When you put a descriptive label on the type of person you are, you're better able to see how you affect others. For instance, we're working with an accounting firm where many of the partners are Sensors, according to the MBTI; they're very good with details, data, and facts and are practical and short-term focused. In the past, this is exactly what most of their clients needed. Now, however, their client base is changing along with the services they offer. A significant percentage of their clients are entrepreneurs who are passionate about their business and value strategic business planning advice. It's very difficult for many of these Sensors to become excited about an entrepreneur's vision and understand how their passion and energy move the business forward. These accounting partners keep focusing on facts and figures, while the entrepreneur is asking them to think conceptually. The accounting partner doesn't understand what he's doing wrong and why the entrepreneur is dissatisfied. After all, the accountants saved them a substantial amount of money in taxes. What else do they want?

Like many other people we've worked with, the partners in this firm didn't grasp the effect of their style on others initially. For years, they had taken their style for granted; they had assumed it was positive. By giving them insight into their personality type and how it contrasts with a client's type, they begin to understand that there's a disconnect and are motivated to make changes so they don't harm their customer relationships.

[1]CDR Assessment Group (1998), Tulsa, Okla.

12

Personalizing Leadership

L eadership can be coached, but it can't be taught as a set of specific skills or behaviors. As useful as leadership development
programs are in helping people learn how to be successful executives, they aren't up to the challenge of personalizing the process.
By *personalizing*, we simply mean that each individual brings his
or her own baggage and assets to the leadership task at hand, each
faces different environmental concerns, and each works for an organization with its own definition of leadership.

Put another way, personalizing leadership means matching an
individual's leadership beliefs and behaviors to the way in which
the organization wants him to lead.

Performance breakthroughs and transformations in this area
can't be accomplished just by helping a person be more honest,
forceful, visionary, or courageous. In years past, leadership training set up a model of these leadership qualities and basically said
to participants in the program, "Learn these and make them your
own." This training approach ignores the reality of a diversified,
constantly changing organization. In a world where people don't
blindly follow positional authority, leaders can no longer tell people
what to do. They need to learn to motivate a diverse workforce
and to motivate them in many different ways. Organizations are
becoming increasingly aware that the old, patriarchal, white-leader
model is not relevant for a majority of their workforce and that the

prototypical leadership qualities don't resonate with women, blacks, GenXers, and employees from Third World countries.

Companies are also recognizing that they don't want everyone to be the same type of leader. They realize that not only does Mary's personality make it impossible for her to fit the old leadership model, but if she is to be successful in leading a recently acquired company, she needs to lead with tact, sensitivity, and an intuitive sense of fairness. This same company, however, may require Laura to lead with an iron will and an ability to balance short-term results with long-range planning. All this translates into different leadership styles for different company needs.

In the leadership area, our coaching focus is to find a fit between who someone is and what someone does, between how an individual defines who he is and how an organization defines what it wants done.

Congruency Between Belief and Action

The first question people ask of their leaders today is, "Can I trust you?" People distrust leaders who take contradictory positions, don't walk the talk, seem to be acting purely out of self-interest, and are deliberately misleading people in order to achieve their own ends. For instance, many leaders issue value statements designed to inspire and guide work behaviors. Many times, these statements involve respect toward others, teamwork, customer focus, quality, innovation, and so on. These statements raise expectations; when they're not met, morale and motivation suffer. For instance, a leader declares how important teamwork is to her company, but organizational incentives only reward individual performance. Or a leader insists that the company prizes innovation above all else while managers routinely punish people who take risks that don't pan out. Or a leader talks about how much he values input from others but frequently disregards that input and does exactly what he feels is right.

Aristotle said that integrity comes from knowing yourself, and this self-knowledge is essential for effective leadership. When people are out of touch with their own feelings, values, needs, and weaknesses, they sometimes "act them out" on others. This acting-out process can take many psychological forms, from denial to projection, but the upshot is that they act in ways that often alienate, disappoint, or anger others. Just as important, when people don't know themselves, they're not leading at peak capacity. A great deal of their energy goes into denying a weakness or trying to get a personal need met, and thus they're distracted from the larger organizational goal. Instead of working to create synergies between two merged companies, leaders focus on getting their need for power met or denying that they're threatened by new policies and ideas emanating from the merger.

All this isn't to say that self-awareness is the only key to effective leadership. Reading the business and workplace environment, forming and selling a vision of the future, and implementing strategies are all crucial. But it's tough to do these things effectively without a keen awareness of how your beliefs influence your actions. For instance, a leader might believe that "style is valued over substance" in his organization. Consequently, he spends a great deal of time and effort on how things look— office decor, glitzy presentations, the way his people dress and present themselves—and relatively little time brainstorming and coming up with substantive concepts and strategies. Because this leader's belief in style over substance is unconscious (he may be aware that stylish presentations are important to him, but he would deny that they're more important than what the presentations are about), he isn't aware of the impact that belief has on his performance. Instead of knowing who he is as a person and using that knowledge to shape his leadership ability, he's being pulled in directions that may not be good for his people or the organization.

Here are some common leadership issues that require coaching interventions:

- *The leader isn't perceived as authentic.* Many times the problem is that people are trying to fulfill a leadership role—a role that may be light years removed from who they are as people. They feel they need to embody particular traits now that they've been promoted or given increased responsibility. The coaching need is for them to be themselves. People can spot phonies in a second and are far more intolerant of them than in the past. Leaders used to be given more latitude, and a certain amount of acting was both expected and accepted. As a coach, you need to identify the behaviors that seem false to others and help clients understand why they're acting in an unauthentic manner.

- *The leader does not appear to be empathetic.* We've talked about empathy at length in our chapter on relationships. As important as this quality is to any manager, it's doubly important to a leader. We hear complaints that an executive is unable to connect with his people and that he doesn't understand them. Our job is to help them first get in touch with who they are and then get in touch with who their people are.

- *The leader exhibits a blissful ignorance of who he is and how he affects others.* These are tough people to coach. They often are extraordinarily confident in themselves and believe they've solved all their emotional problems. In reality, they are self-awareness atheists: they don't believe they have any hidden parts of themselves or that there's a point to figuring out their internal motivation for a given action. As a result, they do great damage to others, fall short of goals, and are supremely confident that the problem always exists on the outside, never on the inside.

- *The leader needs to be in control.* Many times, these people mirror the controlling cultures of former employers or are stuck in old-paradigm thinking. They are dead-set against surprises and risks and wholeheartedly in favor of planning and predictability. Management may recognize that this type of leader is wrong for what the organization wants to accomplish and that they need leaders who take risks and are comfortable with uncertainty and change. Most of all, companies want leaders who take bold action, and they want coaching to help them address the control issues that make them indecisive.

- *The leader has been thrust into a role for which he is unprepared.* People still get promoted into leadership positions for functional success. The best salesperson is chosen to head a company's entire sales region, or the most brilliant researcher is promoted to the top R&D spot. What helped a person excel functionally might not help benefit him as a leader. Coaching, therefore, is designed to help these people transition to a new role. In purely functional roles, they didn't need much self-awareness. They're technocrats. But suddenly, the organization is asking them to inspire and energize others, not just themselves. This is where personalized leadership comes in. Coaching helps them figure out who they are and how they might use their particular beliefs and abilities as a leader.

- *The leader lacks a sense of purpose.* Some people are just going through the leadership motions. They may put on a good face but what they're thinking is, "Why am I doing this?" In these instances, they aren't motivated to work harder, more innovatively, or with vision and excitement. Coaching can help people rediscover their purpose and reenergize them. Part of personalized leadership means being cognizant of one's particular purpose. Once managers understand that purpose, they can make decisions—both work and career decisions—based on whether that purpose is being met. See Exhibit 12.1 for a summary of leadership issues.

This last coaching strategy reminds us of a client who was on the verge of resignation when we were called in. Jack was a top executive leading a major change effort, and his boss was worried that he was dispirited and about to depart. We began coaching Jack, who confirmed that his boss's suspicions were correct. Not only was the difficulty of making change happen depressing him but so was all the political in-fighting surrounding the change effort. He

Exhibit 12.1. Common Leadership Issues.

Issue	Coaching Strategy
Leaders who aren't perceived as authentic	Leaders who seem phony need to be encouraged to be themselves.
Leaders who do not appear to be empathetic	Leaders who don't connect with people need to be coached to get in touch with who they are and then in touch with direct reports as people.
Leaders who are blissfully ignorant of their impact on others	Leaders who are not self-aware and think they've solved all their personal issues need to be given hard-hitting feedback to see themselves as others do.
Leaders who need to be in control	Leaders who hate surprises and are uncomfortable with risk need to be encouraged to take small, bold steps and expect imperfection, which leads to greater courage to let go of control.
Leaders who have been thrust into roles for which they are unprepared	Functional performers with little generalist background need to see the bigger picture and delegate functional activities.
Leaders who lack a sense of purpose	Leaders who are just going through the motions need to reconnect with their larger purpose in their work.

complained that no one seemed to appreciate his efforts and that his management style was under attack by subordinates. Even his boss, he said, was not supportive. Worst of all, Jack felt like what he was doing was "stupid and meaningless."

The real issue, however, was that he had forgotten his purpose in coming to the company; he'd forgotten even earlier goals about why he had decided to go into this particular industry. As we talked, we helped him refocus on his desire to find a position in which he could have a positive impact on thousands of lives. He had always loved the opportunity to shake things up and create something new. His greatest joy as a manager was to help people learn new ways of doing things.

One of the coaching techniques we used was to help Jack imagine what might happen if he actually did resign: "Picture yourself on the golf course a month from now. How will you feel about leaving the company? Will you second-guess yourself and wonder if you might have pulled the change effort off if you had done X and Y? Will you feel defeated and wish you had another chance?"

Eventually, Jack reconnected with his purpose and didn't resign. He saw that he was reacting to temporary setbacks rather than the job itself. His statement that his work was stupid and meaningless really translated into, "At the moment, work feels stupid and meaningless because things are moving so slowly and there isn't a lot of positive feedback." In fact, Jack admitted that his job still provided him with the chance to help people learn and to shake things up — a chance that he might not get elsewhere.

Quite frequently, coaches need to work with budding leaders — people who are placed in leadership crucibles for the first time. Organizations are counting on these neophytes to come through, even though they lack the leadership experience that would help them immeasurably. In lieu of that experience, coaches are called in, and the following case history will detail the process that is used in this type of situation.

Mark's Case: Leading People Toward the Door

The first major leadership challenge of Mark's career involved disbanding his company's computer division and helping most of the division's eight thousand employees make graceful exits. Mark, the financial officer of the division, was named president after his organization was involved in a multibillion-dollar merger with another computer company. Because there were many redundant functions, management decided to phase out the division over time. Mark's job was to do this in a way that met organizational financial targets, retained key employees, and didn't disrupt the rest of the company from a morale or productivity standpoint. On top of this, the political climate in the company was tense and Mark had never disbanded an organization before.

We were brought in to coach Mark, not because of any problematic behaviors management was concerned about but because they anticipated his need to grow into this leadership position. They hoped that we'd be able to facilitate his development, especially given the demands of the assignment. What we did was focus on four key issues.

First, we helped Mark identify his strengths and weaknesses. From feedback we received, it was clear that Mark was considered a solid financial officer, but there were questions about his ability to break out of his financial silo and think holistically. In addition, there was a sense that his conservative personal style might work against him as a leader. Not only did he lack charisma but some people considered him dull.

Second, we worked with Mark on developing a vision of how a successful outcome might look—what factors or measures would indicate that he'd done an effective job of disbanding the division. Third, we helped Mark develop a plan to implement this vision. Fourth, we coached Mark through the actual implementation of the plan.

Mark responded extraordinarily well to this coaching, and his actions flowed directly from his beliefs. As a result, people responded positively and even enthusiastically to his direction, knowing that he was sincere and trying to do the best job possible under the circumstances. He never tried to compensate for his lack of charisma and went about his business in a low-key fashion. His empathy for the people who were going to lose their jobs was heartfelt, and this defused much of the anger that might otherwise have disrupted the company. Mark was also eager to accept help; he knew what he didn't know and assembled a team of people to provide the experience and expertise he lacked. Perhaps most significantly, he developed a plan that flowed from his sense of purpose. When we talked to him about his purpose, he was clear that he took great pride in doing things right, in setting new standards for the way things should be done. In his own quiet way, Mark derived great satisfaction from putting his own stamp on his work. The plan that he developed reflected these ideas; he told everyone that he wanted to manage the dissolution of the division in a way that would serve as a model for other companies. He challenged his people to deal with the situation professionally, emphasizing that they all stood to benefit if they could reach their financial targets and dismantle things smoothly.

In the end, Mark's leadership was considered brilliant. His bosses were tremendously impressed, not only by how he handled himself but how he surpassed their expectations for the disbanding of the division. He exceeded all of his goals, from financial objectives to employee retention targets.

Three Key Steps to Coaching Leaders

Whether you're coaching someone like Mark who is emerging as a leader or a veteran executive who has been in leadership positions for years, three criteria or steps should be kept in mind. Although these steps are important for all coaching assignments, they're especially critical for leaders who frequently fail to take the following steps:

Foster Insight and Understanding

The more responsibility and influence you accumulate and the higher you rise within an organization, the easier it is to lose sight of your strengths and weaknesses and how others perceive you. High-achievers are often reluctant to change unless they receive startling information about where they're falling short or where they need to develop new skills. The shock of sudden insight motivates them to change.

As a coach, you can deliver this "shock" by sharing 360-degree feedback with them or talking about how others perceive them in specific situations. Sometimes this is enough to motivate high-achievers to move in a new direction; their inherent desire to achieve makes them more willing than most to listen to the feedback and make changes.

Insight and understanding don't have to be fostered instantly. Reflecting, meditating, keeping a journal, or simply talking about one's feelings and experiences can yield valuable insights. From a coaching standpoint, you want to encourage people to become *mindful* (a Zen term) about their feelings, reactions, dreams, and nightmares. How do they feel in certain situations? What circumstances cause them to feel that way? What happens to these feelings over time?

Many individuals in management positions are used to looking outward, not inward. That's fine; you want people to keep an eye on organizational or business goals. But when these executives ignore internal issues, they often fall short of organizational goals. When they lack insight about why they do something, they're unable to change the behavior that causes them to fall short of business goals.

Watch for defensive reactions to your questions and in your discussions with clients. Defensiveness may seem like a negative reaction, but it's the precursor of insight and understanding. Most often, people are defensive because of their fear of failing. Many leaders and prospective leaders are terrified of not being in control and of being unable to prevent things from going off course. If you find clients protesting too much when you discuss areas that make them feel vulnerable or that reveal imperfections, explore these areas with them. If you can get someone to acknowledge his imperfection and accept his vulnerability, he'll gain a valuable insight about himself.

Hubris blinds many leaders to their weaknesses. They believe themselves to be invincible and destined for great things. Leaders in the past were afflicted with hubris, but back then self-awareness was less important for leadership. Now, arrogance and posturing is a turn-off to many employees and prevents leaders from empathizing with their people. As in the Greek tragedies, hubris really is a fatal flaw for those who would otherwise be heroes. When leaders suffer from excessive pride, coaches are in a good position to poke and prod this inflated image and help them understand who they are at their core.

We have a client, the head of a large organization, who has a huge office with a beautiful view and a helicopter, plane, and limousine waiting to take him places. People cater to his needs; even his top assistants seem reluctant to disagree with him. Everyone laughs at his jokes and compliments him on his ideas. In this environment, it is very easy for him to ignore the insights that might help him do his job better or stop him from making mistakes. Although he claims that he has cronies in the company who will level with him, his behaviors suggest that either they're not leveling or he's not listening. Many employees view him as isolated and out of touch, and his isolation has caused him to make a number of decisions that he might not have made if he had had more input. High turnover rates can also be attributed to his isolation. Coaching can open his eyes to what's happening; we can tell him things that others are unable or unwilling to tell him. Perhaps most relevant from his perspective (and the reason he brought us in), we can show him how his lack of awareness creates problems that ultimately hurt productivity. Even though this CEO may not care about understanding his subconscious motivations, he is eager for insights about how he may be hurting his business.

Help People Take Responsibility

You'll find that many of the people you coach will appear to buy in to the direction in which you're coaching them; they may acknowledge they have a problem or need to develop in a certain way. Intellectually, they may recognize that they have to learn to manage or work differently. Emotionally, however, they're still refusing to accept that this is their issue. They prefer to blame other people or circumstances for the issue they're being coached on.

People in supervisory positions are sometimes quick to absolve themselves of responsibility. They say, "The problem is the economy," "The market is saturated," or "The young people we're hiring today just aren't as loyal as they were in the past." These are typical comments of leaders looking for excuses for substandard performance. Rather than examine what they've been doing to make a bad situation worse — or how they might change to make a bad situation better — they turn themselves into victims of circumstance or of other people.

Help them shift the responsibility focus from others to themselves. You can do this in a number of ways. Sometimes the best way is simply to remind your clients that people are counting on them, that they've chosen to do their particular jobs, and that people have put their faith in them.

Create Commitment to Change

The following formula suggests how people make this commitment within the Action Coaching process:

$$C = D > SQ + F + S$$

Translated, this formula means Change happens when Dissatisfaction is greater than the Status Quo and when a First step is clear and Support is provided. This means you need to help clients see and acknowledge what they don't like about the current situation or how they might make things different and better. You also need to help them create a vision of a better future and a roadmap for getting there. If this isn't done, managers will simply talk about their commitment to change and never do anything about it.

You can move leaders toward this commitment by capitalizing on their innate desire to learn. Learning and leadership go hand in hand, and most people you'll coach will have an intense need to discover new ideas and information. To give them a chance to learn, you must get them out of their I-know mind-set and into an I-don't-know mode. In most work situations, leaders feel compelled to act as if they know everything. You should create an atmosphere in which they're free to drop this pose and learn new things.

Questions are the best tool you have to help people explore what they don't know (see Exhibit 12.2).

Reflecting on these questions is a great way for people to consider other possibilities and become dissatisfied with the present condition. The more they think about and talk (to the coach) about why they're dissatisfied and what other options exist, the more likely they will be to change.

Besides asking questions, you can also explore people's goals for themselves, their careers, and their companies. People on leadership tracks often have been at a job or in the industry for a long time and may have lost touch with their early hopes and dreams. To get where they are today, they've had to make certain compromises. Getting these people to talk about how excited they were when they were hired for their first job or what turned them on about their career choice can illuminate their dissatisfaction. Thinking

Exhibit 12.2. Leadership Coaching Steps.

Leadership Coaching Steps	
Foster insight and understanding	Share feedback from others, promote reflection, work through defensiveness, encourage greater self-awareness, illuminate blind spots.
Help people take responsibility for the situation	Encourage emotional ownership, not just intellectual; help people shift from "them" to "me"; move people from feeling victimized to being proactive.
Create commitment to change	Change happens when dissatisfaction is greater than the status quo, when a first step is clear, and support is provided; capitalize on people's innate desire to learn and explore.

⇩

Questions to Help People Learn and Explore

What would happen if you asked for help in this area that you're not so skilled at?

What's stopping you from requesting a change?

If you quit today, what regrets would you have?

How might you deal with the conflict without resorting to a win-lose posture?

Why do you want to lead, and why should people follow you?

What legacy do you want to leave behind? What do you want people to say about you after you've left your current role?

What are your vulnerabilities, and where could things fall apart?

What can you do to renew yourself? Your team? Your organization?

and talking about these issues can spur them to recapture that excitement and make a commitment that they'll do so.

Finally, some leaders are in desperate need of renewal. They won't make a commitment to change until they recharge their batteries and gain some perspective on the work decisions they're facing. Executives often lose perspective because of the pressures they're under; they work relentlessly and even obsessively without ever stepping back and taking a breath. Leaders in need of renewal can become overly demanding, not see the big picture, and overlook obvious flaws in a strategy.

We've renewed our clients in all sorts of ways. One senior executive was unable to set boundaries; his boss was intrusive, he was too absorbed in the organization's ambitious goals, he had too many demands on his time. We suggested he go on a retreat to a country he loved, which he did. He came back recharged, and he went about his job with much greater passion and sensitivity to the people around him.

Not everyone has the time or opportunity to go on this type of retreat. In these instances, we've prescribed everything from physical exercise to volunteer work. Sometimes we attempt to tie a renewal activity to some aspect of the business. One of our clients was a top executive with a sporting goods company that was marketing a line of clothes to inner-city youths. We arranged for him to work in an inner-city basketball league for a few days, seeing his market in person rather than as reflected in reports. We coached an executive with an oil company that was attempting to become more environmentally aware in its business strategy. We had this particular executive—someone who had spent his adult life in cities and in office buildings—go fishing with us on an Alaskan river.

Once people get in touch with something vital inside of them (the net effect of renewal), they often are much more motivated to try new behaviors and open their minds to new ideas.

The Breakthrough Connection

Personalized leadership starts with self-awareness but doesn't end there. The people we've worked with who have achieved performance improvement, performance breakthroughs, and transformations have done so because they've made the connection between who they are and what their unique organizational role or goal is. Sometimes this latter requirement is lost within the coaching milieu as clients become wrapped up in self-discovery. As a coach, you need to keep reconnecting them with organizational goals and issues. It does no good for them to have insight about their leadership weakness or make a commitment to change unless they factor in organizational realities.

For instance, when we worked with Mark, the division head who was placed in charge of his division's dismantling, we were constantly focusing his attention on the larger corporate mission. When he talked about his personal conviction and his desire to make sure disbanding the division "was done right," we pushed him to define *right* from both his and the organization's perspective. How would management respond to his ideas about opening new lines of communication with employees about the dismantling? What about his proposal to establish new ways of compensating people (as incentives for doing a good job) during this period? We helped him select a team to facilitate the transition, and in the selection process we didn't limit discussion to who was right for the team (because of their capabilities) but explored the political implications of his choices. Mark kept talking about the measures he had set in place to know whether he'd been successful; we helped him consider measures that the organization would use to judge his success.

Each leadership coaching assignment is different, and the connections that must be made also vary. Mark recognized that to achieve the performance improvement the company required, he needed to think holistically and craft a vision for his people that would give direction and meaning to their work. He didn't have to transform himself from a solid citizen into a charismatic visionary, but he did need to improve aspects of himself to disband the division effectively. This was an easier connection to make than having to transform himself into a charismatic visionary; his ego would have erected roadblocks. The coach's job is much more challenging in an instance like that.

Still, it can be done. With leaders, it often helps to diagram the connection between their personal development needs and organizational requirements. Create a chart that details the following:

- *What the ideal organizational goal is for the client*—what type of leader they want him to become, what they hope this will accomplish, and what the tangible benefits are to a given group (the company, the division, the team) if your client achieves this goal.
- *The level of change required.* Is self-awareness sufficient or is it just a first step? Is performance improvement, breakthrough, or transformation necessary? Why is the agreed-upon level necessary to achieve the organizational goal?
- *How your client will have to change and what he must do to achieve this level of change*—what skills he needs to acquire, what attitudes he needs to shift, what behaviors he should modify. What mileposts signify that he's making progress in his development toward achieving the organizational goal?

This process of connecting individual requirements with organizational goals would be much simpler if there were a universal set of skills that would allow people to become great leaders. In fact, many leadership development programs operate on this premise: assume that people can be trained to be leaders by learning how to develop strategies, visions, communication skills, and the like. Although these skills are important, they may not be important for a particular individual in a particular organization. The skills a leader needs to handle a turnaround are quite different from the ones he needs to lead a mature business. Acting quickly and decisively are crucial in the turnaround, while careful analysis is required in the mature business. Even more problematic is that skill development might not address the real leadership need at all. Most leadership development programs take place in an environment separate from the business—an environment in which the idiosyncrasies of key executives, the cultural imperatives of the company, and the "way things get done around here" aren't factored into the training. As a result, leaders are developed for an ideal rather than a real world. On top of this, an individual may have personal issues that are undercutting his ability to accomplish organizational goals—issues that he may not be consciously aware of.

It's important to take these issues into consideration. The two questions coaches always have to ask themselves are (1) What's preventing my client from becoming the leader the organization wants him to be? and (2) Is the problem inside of him or within the organization or some combination of the two?

Admittedly, there are no simple answers to these questions. Personalizing leadership is not a cookie-cutter approach. But by exploring these questions with clients, coaches can work through the complexities and find the best leadership goals for both the individual and the organization.

13

The Coaching Evolution

The type of coaching that we've described in these pages is not just a product of our particular time and place. Although it's true that the current environment has created a need for coaching that links individual awareness with organizational goals, this need will grow. We'd like to give you a sense of why and how coaching will become increasingly important in the coming years. To that end, we'll talk about the trends that will drive the expansion of coaching programs in every type of organization.

We'd also like to leave you with a sense of what has to be done to make coaching an integral part of the organizational culture. Some cultures are still resistant to coaching — at least the type of Action Coaching that results in performance breakthroughs and transformations. This can be scary stuff, and as a result some companies offer active or passive resistance to coaching. Certain steps need to be taken to inculcate this process and support it, and we'll suggest what managers and leaders can do.

Finally, we want to emphasize what you can do to become a great Action Coach. In the near future, this will be a requirement for just about every manager. It won't simply be a useful skill to have; it will be an essential competency — one that organizations will increasingly prize and base hiring and selection decisions on. If this seems like hyperbole, consider the trends that will make coaching as important a skill as any in the managerial repertoire.

Eight Trends That Will Increase the Value of Action Coaching

The following trends are in different stages of gestation. Some are in full flower; others are just starting to emerge. Let's examine each of them and see how they're making coaching an imperative for every manager.

The Push for Performance

As vigorous as this push is today, it will become even more insistent in the future. The global economy is one well-recognized factor behind this trend, and all the signs point to increased competition from more and more global players. Up and down the line, organizations are asking their people to do more and to do it faster, with greater innovation and flexibility. That's asking a lot, and as more competitors with access to cheap labor and new technologies enter markets, companies will ask even more.

Action Coaching is capable of bringing about quantum leaps in performance. Although performance improvements are nice, performance breakthroughs and transformations are what more and more companies are demanding. The coaching we've been talking about is not just to help people make tiny, incremental changes that will have minimal impact on their work performance. The organizations we work with have highly ambitious goals for their people, and they expect coaching to help them achieve these goals.

Mass Customization of Learning

We're already seeing the deemphasis of one-size-fits-all training, and this trend will pick up steam as organizations recognize the value in the individuality of its leaders, managers, and customers. This point is being driven home in a number of ways. First, training programs are failing to help people deal with change initiatives.

Change affects people differently, and programs need to account for an individual's response to change or they won't work. Second, customers are demanding to be treated as individuals. People expect hotels, car rental services, banks, and other "suppliers" to know who they are, what they require, and what they prefer. Organizations are witnessing the benefits of programs that cater to individual customer needs, and this is helping them change their thinking about their own people. Mass customization in training is the result.

Action Coaching is the perfect way to implement mass customization. Although the actual process doesn't vary from person to person, the implementation takes individual needs and development issues into consideration. It is a high-touch tool that helps people learn new skills, behaviors, and attitudes in ways no formulaic training program can.

The Need for New Growth Catalysts

The old growth catalysts — opening new markets, acquisitions, and so on — are becoming less and less viable. Increasingly, organizations are struggling to find effective growth strategies. In the next few years, growth will come from internal rather than external stimuli. Innovation, breakthrough thinking, and risk taking will be the mainstays of growth, and coaching can create fertile ground in organizations for these qualities to take root in.

Managers who lack self-awareness are typically terrible at motivating others and encouraging them to speak their minds and float "dangerous" new ideas. They're oblivious to the impact of their behavior on others, failing to see that they intimidate people into silence or don't inspire them to take risks.

At the very least, coaching creates this self-awareness. At its best, it helps managers and leaders develop the qualities that foster out-of-the-box thinking and brilliant new concepts, both from these managers and from the people who work with them. Coaching, therefore, helps bring out the ideas that produce growth.

Bewildering Issues Spawned by Stress

A recent study by Aon Consulting Institute documented the increased stress that working people are feeling, and they reported the rather startling finding that 50 percent of workers feel burned out. Everyone is not only being asked to work harder but more innovatively and in new ways (on teams, in foreign countries, on the Internet). As a result, they're angry, confused, and willing to leave organizations for less stressful jobs.

How do managers deal with these people? How can you ask them to do less with more? How can you relieve their stress? How can you secure their commitment when they're under such incredible pressure? How can you help them strike a balance between work and their personal lives?

These issues are tailor-made for coaches, and as stress intensifies in our increasingly competitive, global marketplace, coaches will be the ones who have to deal with them.

The Technology Effect

This effect has been well documented, especially in terms of computers and the ways in which they've made information more accessible up and down the line. Flattened organizations and enhanced communication with customers, distant offices, and vendors are the result of technology. As everyone knows, technology is advancing at such a rate that we can expect even more of an impact in coming years. People will need to learn how to create trust with an on-line team they never meet with. Leaders will have to become comfortable providing a wider range of people with "sensitive" information. We're coaching executives in the Bank of America merger who are attempting to work in vast teams that span many countries and where communication is through teleconferencing, e-mail, and other electronic tools. Each of our clients needs customized assistance in learning how to make decisions and build trust in this new environment.

In addition, technology is blurring the boundaries between customers and suppliers, employees and employers, and one function and the next. Everyone is in the information loop, and there are many opportunities spawned by this connectivity. How do you take advantage of them? How do you become sufficiently comfortable in this connected world to communicate your needs to unfamiliar allies? How do you make others comfortable?

All this requires coaching.

The Search for Meaningful Work

Why am I doing this? is a question more and more employees are asking. As the spirituality movement spreads to the workplace and as baby boomers enter that time in their lives when they begin to question their purpose, existential issues will be raised. Many managers are scared by these issues. They have no training in how to work with people going through a midlife crisis or trying to create a more holistic work-lifestyle.

We've already had a number of clients who were struggling with their own meaning and purpose. They found themselves going through the motions—a job they had once loved to perform had lost its relevance. They needed to reenergize and recommit themselves. Either that, or they had to find another line of work. As coaches, we were able to help them explore these options. They could talk with us in ways they could never talk to their bosses or coworkers.

For managers to help others work through these issues, they have to confront questions of meaning and purpose themselves. Once they resolve them in their own minds, they are in a much better position to coach others.

Rising Development Expectations

Leaders will be expected to develop other leaders, and organizations will be expected to develop their talent in personalized ways. Until fairly recently, these expectations were downplayed. Not so long ago, a request to be coached was considered pushy. Most leaders never had the time or inclination to develop successors and a new generation of leadership; they had more important things to do and figured future leaders would either develop naturally or they'd be hired from other companies.

In the future, leaders who don't develop their people will be guilty of mismanaging a crucial corporate asset. To avoid this possibility, they'll look to coaches to help them acquire this skill. When we coach leaders, we often talk to them about how they might maximize the abilities of their best and brightest people. Coaching is not only working with them to create specific development plans for specific people but establishing an environment in which future leaders can learn and grow—an environment of emotional energy and commitment to the organization.

In one sense, we're predicting that leaders will need to learn to be coaches. Talented people enter companies with explicit or implicit demands to be mentored; they insist on opportunities that will help them acquire marketable skills. Coaching becomes both a recruiting and a retention tool in these situations. Leaders, therefore, will need to be coached in how to be coaches.

An Increasing Emphasis on Diversity

It almost goes without saying that as every organization becomes truly global, every manager is going to have to learn how to work effectively with a wide range of people. It's very easy for people to say they appreciate a diverse workforce and can work with anyone; it's another thing to acknowledge a blind spot that is making it difficult for them to manage people who are different (ethnically, racially, generationally).

In the coming years, we're going to be managing and working with people who are very different from the largely homogeneous groups of the past. Imagine working with a team in which one member is a senior citizen, one is from a Third World country, one is an Ivy League M.B.A., and one is a former housewife who has just rejoined the workforce. You may not realize you have certain biases and beliefs that hamper your managerial ability, but they're bound to emerge when working in this type of situation.

Coaching is an effective way of surfacing blind spots, figuring out how they're impeding work performance, and using tools such as feedback, reflection, and action plans to resolve problematic behaviors.

Here's an example of the type of coaching client we expect to see much more of in the future. Jack, an African American, is a high-ranking executive at a Fortune 100 company. Jack's boss, Richard, brought us in to coach Jack, ostensibly because he wanted him to develop certain leadership and communication skills. In reality, the problem was a lack of real communication between Jack and Richard. Richard never felt that he could be completely open and honest about issues with Jack. Richard was used to working with people like himself: over-forty white males who had received M.B.A.'s, grown up in middle- or upper-class American households, and shared certain interests in common. As a result, Richard held back with Jack, and Jack responded in kind. The honesty and openness necessary for a productive relationship was missing. Ultimately, our coaching focused on helping them build that productive relationship. See Exhibit 13.1 for a summary of the trends that increase the value of coaching.

Every Manager a Coach: How Organizations Can Move Toward This Ideal

The growing demand for coaching means that organizations will be faced with an insufficient supply. There are only so many external coaches who can be brought in; companies need to develop their own. More realistically, they need to provide advice, support, and incentives for people who want to become manager-coaches or peer coaches.

The first and most important requirement is buy-in at the top. This doesn't just mean verbal support for the concept of coaching or a few token interventions. Management needs to walk the

Exhibit 13.1. Eight Trends That Increase the Value of Coaching.

Trend	What's Behind the Trend
Push for performance	Increased global competition between companies requires people to do more and do it faster, with greater innovation and flexibility, creating a need for leaps in performance.
Mass customization of learning	Failure of one-size-fits-all training programs, as well as people's demand to be treated as individuals, makes coaching a perfect vehicle for a "mass customization" of training.
Need for new growth catalysts	External factors (for example, acquisitions, new markets) are less viable for growth, making internal strategies (for example, innovation, breakthroughs) more needed, which can all be enhanced through coaching.
Bewildering issues spawned by stress	With 50 percent of workers feeling burned out, managers need new ways to deal with stress in order to retain and motivate people.
Technology effect	Technology and information are creating needs for managers to lead teams and build trust on-line, impersonally and with less control.
Search for meaningful work	Employees want work to be meaningful—more than a paycheck—and managers need to learn how to work through these issues for their employees and themselves.
Rising development expectations	People expect organizations to provide development opportunities, and companies expect leaders to effectively steward people as assets.
Increased emphasis on diversity	In a global marketplace, every manager needs to identify blind spots and overcome them.

talk. For one of our clients, that meant putting its sixty top people through Action Coaching. Another client provided a more dramatic demonstration of support. The CEO of one of the world's largest companies called a meeting of two hundred top executives and shared his personal experience of being coached. He related much of the feedback he'd received—not all of it positive—and how he was responding to it. His candor made a tremendous impression on the executives, and when he offered them the opportunity for coaching, many of them were eager to take him up on his offer.

Support can take other forms. Sharing key information with a coach is crucial. This might mean discussing organization trouble spots that are having an adverse effect on the client's development or new change initiatives that affect the coaching goal for the client. Support can also involve being responsive to a coach's requests or suggestions. If a coach feels the need to involve other people (bosses, coworkers, and so on) in the coaching process, the organization should make them available. If the coach believes that an individual can best meet development goals by being transferred to a new position or being assigned to a specific project, the organization should do everything possible to accommodate these requests. In other words, the organization should be part of the coach's team rather than view itself as separate from the process.

It also helps when coaching is recognized and rewarded by the organization. Although coaching makes intuitive sense to some managers and they will acquire this skill on their own, others need a push. Sometimes this push is nothing more than being exposed to the positive impact of coaching; for example, one manager sees how another manager used it to help his people improve their performance. A company that formally recognizes and communicates the impact of coaching in newsletters or over the Internet spreads the news about coaching and gets others interested and involved. Perhaps the most motivating way of recognizing and rewarding coaching is to incorporate people development objectives into performance management systems. We've worked with companies that have done so, and when people are evaluated and compensated based on their coaching skill, it quickly becomes part of the culture.

Certainly some managers are natural coaches and can pick up the process quickly and implement it without much help. Reading this book may be all that's necessary. Other people, however, need some training. A coaching-focused training program should be designed to help people develop the diagnostic skills and techniques we've discussed, as well as give them the opportunity to become more self-aware. They'll not foster self-awareness in others until they can do so in themselves.

Perhaps the following is an obvious point, but it bears renewed emphasis: *management needs to view coaching as a broad-based rather than a narrowly focused tool.* There are still executives who perceive coaching to be a quick fix for broken people or a last resort for managers who are in trouble. As a result, they don't take advantage of the developmental possibilities of coaching or they restrict coaching to a small segment of the employee population. For instance, we've found that CEOs and other organizational leaders benefit from coaching as much if not more than other managers.

Finally, and most important, organizations should position coaching as an organizational tool and not just an HR plaything. There are a number of ways management can make sure coaching links with organizational goals. At Levi-Strauss, specific development needs of high-potentials are identified in succession planning meetings, and coaching is integrated into the planning. Coaches are briefed on the developmental needs of individuals in terms of how they fit with organizational concerns. Coaches are expected to keep the organizational target in mind as they work with clients on their issues. In this way, people are developed to benefit the organization as well as themselves.

How You Can Prepare to Become a Good Action Coach

Action Coaches are made, not born. Most of you reading these words have the capacity to become manager-coaches. Although it would be nice to receive organizational support and training in your quest to develop coaching skills, you can do a great deal on your own. Remember, you don't need a doctorate in psychology or years of trying to understand the human psyche to be an effective coach, at least from an Action Coaching perspective. As we've emphasized, good coaches aren't simply self-awareness generators. Instead, they're well-rounded human beings and multiskilled managers who are good at establishing trusting, communicative relationships.

You don't have to wait until someone tells you to develop your coaching skills. You can do a great deal on your own to enhance your value to an organization, as well as your effectiveness as a manager (not to mention your own career advancement possibilities) by developing the ability to do the following:

- *Adopt another person's point of view.* This is as opposed to forcing your point of view on others. Too often, we see managers and even other coaches who are only successful in getting others to do what they want. People want to please their managers and coaches and so forsake their own points of view. As a result, there's no emotional commitment or energy; work might get done, but it doesn't get done well or with much creativity. Good coaches make an effort to understand another person's frame of reference. They appreciate the unique motivations, perceptions, and talents of individuals, and they respect the differences between themselves and others. At the same time, they know that a given point of view may present challenges for the person they're coaching, and they accept that it's going to be a struggle for that person to grow and develop.

If you can empathize with people and see the world through their eyes, you'll be much better able to establish a connection with the people you're coaching.

- *Provide the opportunity for self-motivation.* This is a complex skill, and we're not defining it in the traditional sense of a manager who uses carrot-or-stick techniques to get people to perform. In fact, motivation and coaching are often thought to be mutually exclusive. The role of the manager is to motivate, and the role of the coach is to create self-awareness—and never the twain shall meet. One thing that makes Action Coaching different, however, is that self-awareness and motivation are joined at the hip. Coaches are effective when they discover the key that prompts someone to take action—to change attitudes and behaviors. The motivation does not come from something a coach does as much as from what he makes possible for a client to do. By raising self-awareness and creating a plan to follow, coaches make it easier for individuals to act on what they learn about themselves.

Therefore, concentrate on helping your people discover who they are and giving them alternatives and paths that they can use to do something about what they discover.

- *Develop your own point of view.* One of the paradoxical aspects of coaching is that you need to have your own point of view, as well as be able to adopt someone else's. Coaches aren't neutral or objective. They bring value to the process by expressing their values and ideas about how good organizations work and how effective employees perform. As coaches, we often explain to our clients how strong leaders function, how people produce results, what's fair (and what's unfair) in boss-direct report relationships, and so on. These ideas reflect our values and beliefs; they provide our clients with a direction to move toward. Some clients don't agree with our values and beliefs, and if these conflicts are irreconcilable, we stop coaching them. Most of the time, however, this point of view energizes the relationship between coach and client and provides a sense of what's right and wrong, what's good and bad, to guide someone's actions.

- *Figure out what you believe.* What is an appropriate and effective way for people to behave in your company? Set up your own organizational moral code. Define the traits of a superior manager versus an ineffectual one. This will help you establish your own point of view.

• *Learn to read the context.* In many organizations, coaching occurs in a vacuum. Or rather, it takes place without regard to the politics, policies, and culture of a given organization. It's almost as if people are being coached for an ideal world rather than the real world. Good coaches are attuned to their environments and can diagnose what in these environments may be contributing to a client's problem or impeding his development. They understand it's not only important to be aware of what's happening within someone but what's happening within the workplace context.

You need to be perceptive about how things work in your organization: who controls the resources, how they are procured, what the official and unofficial methods are, what types of behaviors and people have always been prized by the culture, and what the taboos are. The more you're clued in to the answers, the easier it will be to determine how organizational context is helping or hindering your client.

• *Develop a range of communication styles.* Some coaches adopt the classically neutral style of a traditional therapist. Although this style may be effective in certain situations, it's ineffective in many others. Manager-coaches need to practice being confrontational, compassionate, assertive, and open. As this book indicates, people face a staggering variety of challenges and opportunities. Although sometimes coaches need to cut through the blather and force a client to deal directly with an issue, other times they simply need to listen and ask questions. Being able to move from style to style as the situation dictates is a tremendous coaching attribute.

You may have a favored style of communicating. We're not suggesting that you give this up as much as that you add to your repertoire. Practice different communication styles with people you counsel and become familiar with what works and what doesn't.

• *Focus on defining organizationally linked goals.* What happens if your client becomes more self-aware, has a performance improvement or breakthrough, or is transformed? How does this individual's change relate to a specific business agenda? As a coach, it's all too easy to lose the larger focus and get wrapped up in the individual's issues. You may help a manager become more aware of her tendency to bark orders, or you may assist someone else in breaking through planning difficulties, but to what end? Is being a kinder, more considerate manager going to help a manager's group operate more profitably?

These linkages aren't always easy to make. To make them more apparent, you need to explore the linkage in your own mind as well as with the people you're advising. This requires a conscious effort, a resolve to step back from the individual situation and reconceive it based on organizational concerns. If you do this enough, it will become a reflex rather than a stretch.

See Exhibit 13.2 for a test to see whether you would be a good coach.

Exhibit 13.2. Self-Assessment: Becoming a Good Coach.

To what extent do I:	Low				High
Adopt the other person's point of view?	1	2	3	4	5
Provide the person with the opportunity for self-motivation?	1	2	3	4	5
Develop my own point of view? Be clear about my biases, and state my views when appropriate?	1	2	3	4	5
Learn to read the context of the person's and the organization's situation?	1	2	3	4	5
Develop a range of communication styles?	1	2	3	4	5
Focus on defining organizationally linked goals?	1	2	3	4	5

The Well-Coached Organization

In the past, coaching was confined to a small number of individuals who exhibited problematic behaviors. Most of these people were talented but troubled, and they often held important but not top-level jobs. Interventions usually involved an external coach who came in, worked on their personal development, and left.

This concept of coaching has changed, and it will change even more in the future. On the most basic level, these changes involve who coaches and who is to be coached. In terms of the latter, we're going to see a rapid expansion in who is considered coachable. Instead of just problematic people, coaching clients will include individuals who simply need to develop a skill or mind-set that the organization deems important. Instead of just a handful of middle managers, clients will include young managers not long out of school, as well as CEOs and other corporate leaders who recognize that they can better help the organization execute its strategy if they go through the coaching process.

The notion that an individual employee is a company's greatest asset has become a tired slogan, but it's one that is going to be reinvigorated by the trends discussed in this chapter. The grim realization that cookie-cutter training doesn't work and the hope that customized counseling will work is making coaching a more democratic discipline. As growing numbers of organizations come to this conclusion, coaching will spread throughout the ranks.

As this happens, it will be essential to have more and different types of coaches. External coaches will be used for top executives and in other situations where an in-house coach would feel uncomfortable; external coaches will also be called in because they possess a particular expertise (for example, coaching leaders through transitions) or to train other coaches. Internal coaches will focus on coaching assignments where in-depth organizational knowledge is required. An internal coach will not be the boss of the person being coached. Peer coaching is becoming more common, and it involves coaching among organizational equals. But internal coaches might also perform a separate function within an organization; they may be people whose only responsibility is to coach others. Their value is as "objective insiders," that is, people who understand the system but are not an integral part of it. The third and fastest-growing group will be manager-coaches. They will deal with the most common problems and development opportunities their people face.

Ultimately, what all this coaching is predicated on is the increasing value of the individual to the organization. As we continue to downsize and flatten our organizations—and as organizations achieve relative parity in other areas—an individual's contributions are magnified. The company that routinely helps its people achieve performance breakthroughs and transformations is the company that will gain a competitive edge. Although individuals can achieve these breakthroughs and transformations on their own, having the assistance of an Action Coach facilitates the process immeasurably.

Index

Emotional inconsistency. *See* Hyper-
moody people
Emotional intelligence, 207–210,
219, 221
Emotional ownership, 248, 250
Emotions: in conflict situations, 184,
185; helping clients understand,
214–215, 216–217, 220, 246; out-
of-control, 212–213; in relationships, 212–213, 214–215,
216–217, 220
Empathy: behavior problems and,
100; client, for boss, 175; in
coaches, 49–50, 51, 265; for
conflict management, 196–198,
204–205; in leaders, 240, 242; as
organizational requirement, 99–
100, 207; relationship skill of,
207–210, 219, 221
Enthusiasm, as reaction to coaching,
132
Entitled workforce, 159
Environment. *See* Context; Organizational culture; Reading-the-
environment skill
Evaluation: of boss-client relationship, 166–168, 169, 173–174; in
case examples, 55; of changed
situations, 150–155; checklist for,
47–48; of client-coach relationship, 151; in Step 8, 45–48, 78–
80; of tools and techniques, 151–
155; tools and techniques for,
78–80. *See also* Assessment
Executive coaches: coaching task of,
9; defined, 7
Existential gaps, 116
Existential issues, 259, 262
Expectations: customer, 225–226,
227–228, 232–233, 234–235; establishing mutual, in Step 2,
38–39, 65–66; raised by leaders,
238; in relationships, 215–216;
techniques for establishing, 65–66
Experience, gaining depth through,
160
Experts, involving, 154–155, 205

External coaches: coaching task of, 9;
defined, 8; need for, 269

F

False advocates: change management
problems of, 104; in complex environments, 98; conflict-collaboration problems of, 190; described,
94–95, 96; tips for coaching, 95
Favoritism, 170, 204–205
Fear: as cause of uncoachability, 148;
of conflict, 184; overcoming, 148;
as reaction to coaching, 130–131,
132; of worriers, 90
Feedback: anonymous, 157, 170; for
boss-client relationship, 167, 171,
176; boss's refusal to provide, 171,
176; for breaking through denial,
144, 157–158; collection and communication of, in Step 4, 41–42,
71, 72; for conflict-collaboration
problems, 200, 201, 203; from customers, 232–234; for egotists, 86;
importance of, 41; interpreting and
using, 127, 128, 140–141; lack of
honest, 146, 149, 156–157, 161,
168; for leaders, 246; for motivation, 160; multiple sources of, 127,
140–141, 246; negative, confrontation techniques and, 69; positive,
skewed toward, 156–157; real-time,
200, 201, 203; for relationship-skill
problems, 214
Feedback collection, 41; tools and
techniques for, 41, 71, 72
Feedback communication, 42; tools
and techniques for, 41, 71, 72
Feelings. *See* Emotions
Feel-know-do factors, 61, 63
FIRO-B test, 191, 199, 202, 236
First meeting, 125–142; assessment
for, 126–130, 139–141; case
examples of, 125–130, 138–139;
checklist for, 139–142; establishing trust and mutual expectations
in, 38–39; initial reactions to
coaching and, 130–132, 139;

A Strategic Boot Camp for Leadership Development

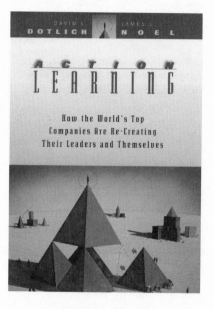

"Action Learning combines coaching, practice, reflection, and doing. It is the future of executive and leadership development."
— Ken Smith, *president,* Wafertech

Action Learning

How the World's Top Companies Are Re-Creating Their Leaders and Themselves

David L. Dotlich, James L. Noel

M ore than just another training program with limited efficacy, Action Learning addresses the wide variety of issues spawned by unrelenting change. It directly links executive development to immediate strategic needs. It touches attitudes and behaviors in ways that support successful organizational transformation. And it can be used to achieve any number of specific business goals. Action Learning gives companies the power to re-create themselves by first re-creating their leaders; and in this book, authors Dotlich and Noel tell readers exactly how they can go about implementing an Action Learning program of their own.